# LIKE FIRE SHUT UP IN MY BONES

David L. Brown

*A BIOGRAPHY—THE EXPOSING OF*
*GOD'S TRUTH IN THE LIFE OF A MAN*

**REV. DAVID L. BROWN**
**8421 CHURCH LANE,**
**CHARLES CITY VA, 23030**
**PHONE: (804) 829-6832]**
**(NONFICTION)**

PRESS

# In Memory

This book is dedicated to the loving memory of my
cousin, friend, and brother in Christ—
Frank Elsworth Christian Jr. "Franky"—1958-2001.
He is greatly missed.

# Table of Contents

# Acknowledgement of Thanks

I would like to acknowledge the people who bestowed Godly influence unto me:

To my Lord and Savior Jesus Christ, who saved my soul from a dying hell, and retained a hedge of protection around me. He gave me grace when I deserved it not, and showed me mercy when wrath was justified.

To my parents, Robert Walker and Rosa Estelle Brown, who sowed the Word of God into my spirit, and, in my youth, insisted that missing Sunday school was never an option.

To my grandmother, Erselle Jones, who stayed up praying weekend nights while we were out partying. She considered not sleep until we were home safe. At times, grandma blessed us with the privilege of reading scriptures to her as she drifted to sleep.

To my aunt, Shirley P. Jones, who counseled me in the practical use of God's Truth. She has consistently shown herself to be a doer of the Word and not a hearer only.

❧❦

To my loving wife Cathy, who has prayed for and counseled me with all fervency and longsuffering. Jesus said that we are to forgive seventy times seven. But, her forgiveness has exceeded that.

❧❦

To my brother in Christ, Alvin "Pickle" Williams, who has been profitable for me in understanding the scriptures, and to apply it in this present time. Much of my spiritual reflection in this book is the result of his teachings. He was one of the first men, whom I personally knew, who simultaneously displayed a faith talk and a faith walk.

❧❦

To my two genetic and spiritual brothers in Christ, Ricky and Toney, who have proven to be good friends and beacons of right living. In my worst years of rebellion, they never once disowned me as a black sheep. They seemed to believe God on my behalf, and Christ delivered.

❧❦

To my uncles Oatha "Curtis" Jones and Harrison Lee "Dunney" Jones, who always supported my brothers and me in sports. Whether helping to train us by perpetual play during our childhood and adolescent years, or attending many high school football and basketball games, cheering us on to victory. This was particularly special to me because my parents worked mostly at night and couldn't attend games, but our loyal uncles "stood in the gap" in their stead. Also, during those early partying years, they would be found in many of the clubs where we attended, being watchful to keep trouble from us, and to see that we got home safely.

🙙🙛

To my parental in-laws—Stanley and Hilda Cotman, which took on the task of parenting our eldest son Jeff during the years of my running from responsibility. They fed, clothed, and sent him to church. They have assisted my wife in every possible way. My father in-law has displayed a work ethic before me that is truly rooted in selflessness. Though, in the beginning of my marriage, I did not display the proper attitude of duty toward his daughter, never once did he treat me unkind or in a judgmental manner. I thank him for his Christ-like example.

🙙🙛

To my wife's sister, Crystal, and their aunt Mamie— I thank them both for standing in the gap during those years of our marital troubles. They selflessly cared for our small children and were always ready to help Cathy through the hard times. And as far as aunt Mamie is concerned, she has gone above and beyond what anyone could hope for. She is truly a woman of faithfulness unto the Lord.

# Foreword

May God use this book as a lifeline so that others who are caught in this trap of witchcraft may reach up and grab hold to God's unchanging Word. I pray that the Word will become Fire shut up in your bones. Let the Word transform you into the image that God predestined you to become. As I read this book, I saw how God changed my husband from the inside out. I know God is no respecter of persons, and is willing and able to do the same for you.

*Cathy Brown*

# Preface

This book is not so much a biography as it is an imperfect chronology of events. The purpose of this book is to show the veracity of God's Word being exposed through the life of a man. The Bible says that all the ways of God is judgment, and whatsoever a man soweth that shall he also reap. God's Word is always true, and it is filled with warnings, admonitions, promises, and revelations, which are meant for our benefit. The Bible says in II Timothy 3:16, "All scripture is given by inspiration of God, and is profitable for doctrine, for reproof, for correction, for instruction in righteousness." With each decision a man makes, God's Word covers the reason for the consequences thereof. Thus, this book will show how the scriptures are consistent with the realities of life; therefore, if one chooses the wisdom of the Word, he will have Godly prosperity in all his ways. Remember, it is written that the Word of God is indeed a lamp unto our feet and a light unto our pathway.

## Chapter 1

# First Touch

Lying on the floor against my grandmother's bed, I felt physically tired and filled with fear. Just minutes earlier, I sensed tremendous need to pray for my salvation. I was five years old.

My grandmother, Erselle Jones, sometimes allowed us to play in her bedroom. My brothers and I called her "Big Momma" until 1967, when we began calling her Grandma. Playing alone in her room, riding my hobbyhorse, I imagined fantasies about my future and entertained thoughts of Christmas time and toys. I desired to visit places, such as the big department stores in nearby Richmond, Virginia or the beach, where I had once been at that point in my life. I even imagined such simple things as going with our dad to pick up mother from work at the New Kent Restaurant, hoping she would have some ice cream treats to share.

On this particular day, I sensed a foreboding in my spirit. I knew something was desperately wrong. Feeling a need to pray, I bent my knees to the floor, and speaking that which I felt in my heart, beseeched God to save my soul from a burning hell. I can't remember exactly what I said, but called on the name of Jesus, as I understood Him at that age. I had a distinct feeling of fear. Not the fear of something evil or satanic, as I often felt at night, but a fear of God's power. My prayer was fervent and sincere. I prayed with all my soul (this was before I knew that one should pray with effectual fervent prayer) and all my strength, to the point of sweating. Those summer days were hot and humid, with no hope of relief.

My submitting to this compelling to seek God's face resulted in a peaceful fatigue that was complemented by joy and inner warmth. Somehow I knew I was with God, and that He was with me.

Another strange thing occurred: I sensed a moving presence causing change within me. There was something being planted —a seed. Even then, I knew that it was a seed of "AFFECTION" for the Lord. Also it was as though I had new energy and new thinking. I knew, at that point, the Lord would be the common denominator in every small and great thing that would happen in my life.

## Chapter 2

# The Fear of God

Often, as a small child I was taken to church, at least according to my estimation. I sat in fright of the fierce warnings bellowed out by our appearingly angry preacher, and was afraid to fall asleep during services, fearing that the wrath of God would come upon me. However, I often slumbered during worship services.

Reverend Watkins was the first preacher that caused me to attend my hearing to the Word of God. We visited church on Sundays, during revivals, holidays, and other special occasions and programs, including funerals, which was obviously grim. Nevertheless, I desired to find out what God wanted me to know. The only thing that scared me more than the Word of God was my ignorance of it. We were taught, very early in life, certain scriptures to introduce us to the Word. One scripture best describes my beginning walk with Christ, Proverbs 9:10, *"The fear of the Lord is the beginning of wisdom: and knowledge of the holy is under-standing."KJV*

## Chapter 3

# Rocking Heads
# and Funerals

My brother Ricky and I spent our pre-school days watching Captain Kangaroo on the boob tube, during the early 1960's, while sitting in our old and tattered lounge chair. We developed a habit of rocking back and forth in that old chair, vigorously beating our heads against the upper part while moving our torso to and fro. We found this rocking to have a calming effect on our being. However, our grandmother was concerned about this daily routine of head and body bashing. She strongly admonished us to stop. She lamented, while cooking thick, delicious smelling slab bacon; and homemade biscuits, smothered in molasses and cold hard butter, "Daybit and Ricky, stop that rockin, before yawl hurt yourself in the head!" We'd stop for a minute or two, but start again. Grandma would soon call us to the kitchen for breakfast, which was the only thing that pulled us away from the television.

On one particular morning, after breakfast, and continuing our morning television marathon, grandma's sister, aunt Elizabeth, bolted through the front door, crying and screaming franticly "Daddy is dead, daddy is dead!" Until that moment, I had never seen my grandmother cry. Tears streamed down her soft-skinned face, but her weeping was quiet and peaceful. She seemed to be more intent on comforting her sister rather than sharing in the hysterics. Later, I realized that my grandmother, a Christian women, and steadfast in the faith, reacted as the apostle Paul writes in 1st Thessalonians 4:13," *But I would not have you to be ignorant, brethren, concerning them which are asleep, that ye sorrow not, even as others which have no hope."*

I desperately wanted to hug and comfort my grandmother, but could see that my two younger brothers, Ricky and Toney, were afraid. So, we snuggled together in that old tattered chair, with me and Ricky rocking like there was no tomorrow. The rest of that day was sort of lonely and quiet. But shortly after the crying ceased, I somehow knew that everything would return to normal with all haste. On the next day, as I diligently observed my grandma's mood, manner, and demeanor, she acted as if the previous day's events never happened.

I am mindful of another absence in the family during this approximate time in the 1960's. Our grandmother's uncle, whom we called "Uncle Joe", was conspicuously absent from our presence. This was the first time that I had experienced a sense of loss. Though my brothers and I didn't know him well, he sometimes blessed us with his kind words and bubble gum. He would make that one-and-a-half mile trek from his house to Mr. Eugene Major's old country store. Occasionally, my brothers and I waved and hollered greetings to him as he walked by the house, using a walking cane to make his journey, for he was elderly and not of good health. I would eagerly await his return walk home, hoping for at least one gumball. When Uncle Joe died, I was saddened, and greatly missed his presence, though I told no one. Part of my first childhood memories were of him. After his death, I'd sit on our front steps watching the road in both directions, imagining him walking by. I envisioned him beckoning us to run out to the road to retrieve the candies he bought us. Yet still, I knew in my heart he would never come that way again. It is wonderful how a child requires little of people in order to share their love and affection. But, Halleluiah! Due to what I had seen and heard at home and in church, as to God's plan for believers, I obtained peace and confidence that my loss would be restored. Amen!

## Chapter 4

# Rah-Rah the Chubb

*There are some who are the*
*children of disobedience*

I n 1967, our home was visited by a giant burst of hyper-activity, in the person of a seven year old boy cousin, we called Rah-Rah. His family lived in Spring Valley, New York. But, because of the difficulty that my aunt incurred in rearing Rah-Rah, sometimes called "Chubb" or "Chubby", she sent him to live with Grandma. My parents took on the larger task of trying to positively influence him. Chubby's biological father, Uncle Bubba Dick, lived in the same house as us, however he offered no input in the rearing of his son, leaving it to my parents and grandma. I believe that my uncle's silence and non-participatory attitude was pivotal in his son's rebellious behavior. Chubby saw that his father showed no concern for his misdeeds and gross disrespect toward family members, neighbors, and schoolteachers. I overheard my grandmother talk to my uncle about his responsibility to counsel and discipline his son, yet he put forth no effort. Chubby threw himself into every pleasure and whim he desired. His deeds were always mischievous or in rebellion to authority. Some of his antics were gross and disgusting. When Chubby and I were in the third grade, he purposely tore a hole through his left pocket, to expose his erection to the girls in our class. There was one little girl who was aroused as to touch his private part. A boy like this is very dangerous to other children who may be easily influenced.

Chubby had a degree of charisma that was uncommon for a child. He could provoke others to enter into whatever he was scheming. One night, while all adults were out of the house, except our grandmother, he convinced Ricky and me to swing along side him on the top of the entranceway into our den and urinate on the floor. We did this in intervals while grandma moved throughout the house cleaning various rooms. Chubby, not to be undone, went a step further and proceeded to defecate on the floor. The house, being dark at that time of night, did not expose the sight of this grotesqueness, but my grandmother could smell the stench. She thought it was from the pot, which was used for urinating and defecating, for there existed no plumbing in the house.

Due to my parents working odd hours, there was a dramatic decrease in supervision. Our grandmother did her best, but due to the high population count in our home, she was often overwhelmed with housework. Consequently, we were left to our own curiosities and opportunities to experiment with whatever temptations and influences came our way. We sometimes had as many as fourteen people living in the house. There were uncles, aunts, cousins, and siblings, clustered in one house, sometimes sleeping four or five to a bed. This made it easy for us children to get into mischief as the opportunity presented itself.

Along with the decrease in parental supervision, there was an increase in bad behavior, which was provoked by our troubled cousin. He convinced my brothers and I to steal, which we knew was wrong. Yet, it was difficult to resist the pleasure possibilities of our ill-gotten gains. We, at various times, stole from our parents, relatives, the school's teacher's lounge, and once from Kings Department Store. I, though weak in my conviction, was tremendously disturbed in my spirit. However, as I gave in time and again to my cousin's promptings, it became easier for me to do any wrong that resulted in pleasure fulfillments. It did occur to me that Chubby was often preoccupied with doing things that I knew were either sin or conspiracies to do sin. Even in my childish naivetÈ, I sensed an evil spirit with him that seemed to dictate his every thought, action, and reaction. It is written in Ephesians 2:2 that the prince of this world is "...the spirit that now worketh in the children of disobedience". He seemed to abhor doing right. When we did activities that were good and acceptable, I noticed that Chubby was highly uneasy, and bent on turning the activity into an opportunity to do something wicked. For example, we children went out to pick blueberries one day so grandma could make blueberry pies. We looked forward to this treat. The berry plants were high and full, but Chubby came up with the idea to throw rocks at cars that were passing by. According to Chubby, we could get away with this if we hid in the bushes. After a while, only he and I were left to throw rocks, because our cousins, Alphonso, whom we called "Doc, and Clyde, whom we called "Clydy Boy", left for more interesting activities. This was the middle of summer, and the heat was almost unbearable. Yet, Chubby and I remained— probably due to the sometimes competitiveness we experienced between one another. To my regret, this was one of several shenanigans in which I played a part. This foolish endeavor resulted in my breaking a window of a passing car. The screeching sound of those braking tires put a fear in my heart that I had never felt before. Chubby quickly shouted, "Lie down, hide!" The car backed up to search for us. To my surprise, Chubby boldly got up and approached the vehicle with an attitude of innocence and arrogance, and enquired of the driver as to what he wanted. Fearfully hiding amongst the bushes of blueberries, I overheard the driver ask him who threw the rock that cracked his windshield. Chubby stated that he didn't know, but he lived in one of the houses on that road. The driver, whom I never did meet, asked if I was kin to Harrison Jones, and my cousin answered, "Yes". I was mortified!

How could he tell on me? He was supposed to be the one who could hold out longer than any of us. This happened, I believe, in July '68, a time when blacks in the south were still considered to be inferior, second-class citizens to white folk. The driver of the car happened to be a white teenager, who was the son of a large crop farmer. Incidentally, I was bothered by what I had done; feeling guilty, as well as worried about the consequences I was to suffer. Even worse, I became guilt ridden by what I witnessed when that driver caught up with my dad, whom everyone called "Skinny". That teenager, the best that I could discern from a distance, spoke demandingly and demeaning to my dad. He appeared to have no regard that my father was an adult. He should have spoken in a decent and respectful tone. My father responded to the boy's ranting by saying, "If I'm going to pay for that glass, then I'm going to keep it". It seemed that my dad said that to gain some kind of recompense for this boy's racial posture toward him. At that time in my life I didn't know about the social disparities and uneasiness between blacks and whites, but I saw a distinct look of shame on my father's face as he walked back into the house. My mother, who I considered to be somewhat a strict disciplinarian, said very little to me about this incident, and my dad said nothing at all. As I look back, for the remainder of that summer, I felt a kind of sickness in my heart. I sensed a grieving within myself, but didn't know how to deal with it. I avoided looking upon my mother and father for some time, wanting to hide from their presence. I am now sure that the sadness I felt was not mine, but the grieving of the Holy Spirit. The Bible teaches, in Isaiah 63:10 and in Ephesians 4:30 that we can bring grief upon the Holy Ghost, who dwells with us and in us. Also, upon reflection, I realized that I was inwardly chastised of God, because of my need for spiritual cleansing, discipline, and repentance. It is written in Hebrews 12:6 "for whom the Lord loveth he chasteneth."(*KJV*)

Although sporadic, I sometimes sensed a burning within myself to enter into prayer during those childhood days. These prayer moments were done privately; and were sought from the depths of my heart. Even at preschool age, I would physically embrace the Bible, yearning to read it, and sit in wonderment at what it said, knowing that it contained words from God. My grandmother's big Bible contained pictures of Christ and other biblical characters, which increased my desire for God's Word. Yet, this ambition was interrupted many times by temptations to do mischief, which were, more often then not, instigated by our cousin. He remained successful in convincing us that pilfering and vandalism were indeed fun, profitable, and pleasingly satisfying to the appetite.

I would follow after such behavior for a while, until I either got into deep trouble or became vexed by my own sinful deeds. The Bible states, in Hebrews 11:25, that Moses refused to enjoy the pleasures of sin for a season, which suggests that it is possible to become ensnared in gross sin, due to the high level of euphoria afforded by its strong enticements. But, even highly enticing sin would become unsatisfying when one has at once known the pure sweet taste of

God's cleansing presence. I know that it is of a truth, as spoken of in Psalms 34:8 "Taste and see that the *Lord* is good" (NIV).

## Chapter 5

# A Sower Went Out to Sow

*The amoral sexual seed planted into our flesh*

My first sermon, preached in December of 2000, was entitled "The sowing of the seed". The introductory verses were from the Gospel of St. Mark, 4th chapter, in which Jesus explains that the sower, or planter, sows the Word of God, which are spiritual seeds. My premise for this first sermon was that the sower spoken of in the text was not the only sower in the world today, nor were the seeds that were sown by him the only seeds sown in the world today.

I grew up in an area of the community where most youths, with whom my brothers and I associated, were older than us. Though the area kids were always welcoming, their ways were sometimes strange to me. My mother, who was going through positive changes in her life, was becoming spiritually discerning and intuitive about people. She became highly uncomfortable about my brothers and I spending time playing at certain other houses. She preferred we play in our own yard, where strict rules were set, and accomplished, when properly supervised. Nevertheless, we often played with others at their homes; and for a while it was fun-filled, sometimes roughhousing, but usually innocent. However, lascivious behavior was craftily exposed through the introduction and teaching of pornography. An older boy in our general neighborhood had caught the bug of pornographic obsession, and he was hooked. Young boys harboring porno magazines were not uncommon, but were then and now highly dangerous to their lives, future families, and to society as a whole. Pornography is now known to be the root of many temptations to commit sexually related crimes, such as rape, child molestation and abduction, as well as sexually perverted behaviors such as homosexuality, bisexuality, and pedophilia, which is the caressing of a child for sexual fulfillment. It is this behavior of which I almost became a victim. Excitably, this pre-teen would secretly show neighborhood kids the enticing pictures displayed in his triple "X" rated magazines. We became overwhelmed with desire for sexual gratification. I began to look at females from a different perspective. Girls, at this very early age of my life, became objects of sexual fantasy. But, I was blindsided by a different agenda of this older male youth. One day, oblivious to his motives, he asked me to follow him into his bedroom. Being six years old, I expected us to play with toys. He received fun things for Christmas, as well as on other occasions, that our parents either couldn't afford or didn't approve of, such as "bee-bee guns", mini-bikes, chemistry sets, and magic tricks. But on this occasion I was thrown for the loop of my life. He approached me in a very disturbing manner, asking me to take off my clothes, and get into bed. Shocked and speechless, I instantly entered into a state of utter fright and confusion. I trusted this person unconditionally, because, up to that point, he had never treated me less than kind, and was always generous. His family, compared to ours, seemed better off financially, thus, many of us gravitated toward them. It must be understood that this eleven year old boy did not understand the depth of his wrong, although, he knew in his heart, as did I, that this was unacceptable. But, thank God for little sisters. In that moment, one of his sisters came to the bedroom entrance and vigorously insisted that he stop. She continued by threatening to tell our parents if he persisted in this pursuit. After they had a few words, he subsequently exited the room, leaving me there in a state of bewilderment. Again, on another occasion, he tried compelling me, but his sister came to my rescue.

An incident such as this never happened again, and it was approximately thirty years later when I told my parents. Yet, I never harbored any resentment toward this person. I am grateful to my parents and church for teaching me the notion of "forgiveness" at this early age.

Although his perverted attempt was unsuccessful, he could have fostered homosexual behavior into our mist. However, a few years later, other sexual experimentations with the girls of our small community would prove just as emotionally and psychologically deceptive.

## Chapter 6

# Second Touch

*The carnal grip of lust*

Only by the grace of God the attempt of sowing seeds of homosexuality did not take root. I believe this behavior is learned, developed, and nurtured via teaching and exposure to the sexual activity of sodomy, as well as other positions practiced to achieve gay and lesbian sexual gratification. As to the signs of our present times, the apostle Paul writes in 2nd Timothy 3:2-4, *"For men shall be lovers of their own selves, covetous,* boasters, proud, blasphemers, disobedient to parents, unthankful, *unholy. Without Natural affection,* truce breakers, false accusers, incontinent, fierce, despisers of those that are good, Traitors, heady, high-minded, *lovers of pleasures more than lovers of God" (KJV).* Yet, the exposure to such seedings was promptly terminated, through, I believe, intercession from God. It is written in 1st Corinthians 10:13 *"....God is faithful, who will not suffer you to be tempted above that ye are able; but will with the temptation also*

<u>*make a way to escape*</u>, *that ye may be able to bear it"*. Praise God! I was given a way of escape from the abomination of homosexuality. I am convinced that my acceptance of Jesus Christ that day at my grandmothers bed (chpt. 1), created a spiritual protective covering over me, which allowed only those temptations that I **could** withstand, while going through the spiritual processes of being released from unbearable temptations, whatever they may have been. God made it so that the weapon of perverted sexual immorality formed against me would not prosper, AMEN!

Though the attempt at seeding my spirit with homosexual tendencies failed, I succumbed to immoral heterosexual lust for area girls, due to exposure to pornographic materials. My secret desires for them probably stemmed from the fact that they were the only girls with whom I spent time. Children living in Charles City County, in the 1960's, didn't have a lot of opportunities for socializing with other kids, except at Sunday school, or in public schools when there was a great deal more fruitful structure than in our present school systems.

Around 1968, some of us began, heterosexually, experimenting with intimate touching. This was purely carnal curiosity. Kissing the girls, and romantic speaking, never entered into the acts of our foolish attempts. Oddly enough, my brothers never participated in these antics with the area girls, nor did our female cousins, that lived next door. In fact, only my cousins Chubby, mentioned in chapter 3, and Clydy Boy, and I pursued these sexual conquests. Chubby was the prime instigator of these epics. We never had intercourse with the girls, though we tried. The girls would not let us go *that* far in our pursuit. However, they did allow touching, which quickly turned into partial removal of clothing. There were several occasions on which we did this, when finally, the girls ended theirs and our participation in this behavior. Unfortunately, unlike the issue of homosexuality, the stronghold for heterosexual lasciviousness remained in me. This was to resurface at age 16, at which time I entered in what was to be a twenty-plus years tumultuous relationship, with a young, sensitive girl named Cathy, who eventually became, and is still, my wonderful wife. (Further subject matter regarding the development of our relationship will be discussed later.)

## Chapter 7

# Fear

*The master stunter*

Of all the reasons known for a person's underdeveloped emotional and spiritual maturity, fear may be the most prevalent. Fear is contrary to faith, trust, and courage. A person, especially at childhood, who succumbs to sudden and tight-gripped fear, may not, besides physically, enter into the characteristic areas of growth, and flourish, as he ought. A spirit of fear can hamper the processes of emotional, spiritual, psychological, and even intellectual growth.

Fear gripped my mind very early in life.

As mentioned earlier, there were many relatives living in our house, which made the sleeping quarters very crowded. For a while I slept in the same bed with my maternal uncles, Curtis-called "Dirty Bill", Eugene- called "Fisher", Harrison- called "Dunney"; and sometimes joined by my fraternal uncle James Edward, whom we called "Mandy". Sleeping in that queen size bed with them made me a paranoid insomniac. I never had one decent night's sleep while with them. I couldn't breathe, being pressed in from all sides, nor move or turn over to make myself more comfortable. Some slept at the head, and others at the foot of the bed. As stated in chapter 1, I had a habit of rocking my head when sitting in our den chair while watching TV. Well, I also had a habit of rocking my head in bed, by swiftly moving it from side to side. I can't remember when this habit started, but it calmed my fears and helped me fall asleep. However, this activity could not be accomplished among them. Thus, I laid awake night after night in stark fear for my life, which was intensified by fear of darkness. One night I prayed for release from this torture; and God answered. My grandmother got hold of a sofa bed for our den, which became sleeping quarters for my brothers and me, and she moved the television into the living room. My nights were filled with peaceful and restful sleep. The fear of death and night fright subsided.

This relief from sleeplessness remained for a long time, but it did not last. That spirit of fear reared its ugly head yet again. Due to our house's lack of modern facilities, for we used an indoor pot, our susceptibility to vermin was great. Many times we were swamped with mice, which came out in multitudes at night. I found this out the hard way. One night my blissful sleep was interrupted by a strange dream whereby I experienced excessive itching. I scratched up and down my legs and in my groin area without relief. Finally, I awakened, finding mice running up and down my pajama legs. They were in bed with us! This did not awaken my brothers, but I freaked. Fortunately, our grandmother was awake, and sent us to get in bed with our mother. After that incident, our parents bedded us in the floor adjacent to them. But, this solution was short-lived. A few nights later, my mother, in a quiet, yet panicky voice said, "David, Ricky, Toney get up! Get up! Now!" My eyes opened to see a crew of mice scurrying about my head. We quickly jumped into bed with her, while she instructed our father to sleep on the floor. This new sleeping arrangement lasted until we got a little older, then we were given a bed in one of the other rooms. Also, the mice frenzy eventually dissipated. However, this was not the end of my bout with fear.

It was mandated by my grandmother that the women and children use the pot only. However, in my sixth year, grandmother decided I should use the outhouse that was located in the mist of the woodsy area, about fifty feet directly behind our house. One hot summer night, around midnight, I had an urgent need to relieve myself. My grandmother, doing late night cleaning, refused to let me use the pot. She made me go to the outhouse. I tried to hold on until morning, but my bowels would not cooperate, thus I had to enter into the proverbial "valley of the shadow of death". I found that Walking through those dark woods, on that thinly made path, was scary and ghastly. I was horrified! Upon entering the structure, I saw that there were spider webs in every corner of the facility. Due to the spacious gaps between the wallboards, the bright moonlight shone through and allowed me some visibility. Pulling down my "PJ's", I became concerned that I might fall into the hole, because the circumference of the toilet seat was very round, and my derriere was not big enough for even a near fit. Nevertheless, I, with my own strength, upheld myself above the rim. I hurried myself, wiped, and zoomed back into the house with all haste. The next day I related to my mother what had happened; and she proceeded to rebuke my grandmother. I, nor my brothers, never again were to use the outhouse at night. Unfortunately, the seeds of fear had taken root; and were to be an inhibitor in many areas of my life.

## Chapter 8

# A Head Start

Sometime during the summer of 1966, I was enrolled in the Head Start public school program. My mother, called Estelle, with me franticly crying and pulling away, ushered me into the lobby of the school's gymnasium. She did not inform me that I was going to school with other kids that I didn't know; nor would she remain with me. I cried so hard that my eyes must have reddened and swelled. After a very long period of me resisting, I was approached by a very confident and friendly boy, named Lorenzo Washington. This young child proved to be my mother's saving grace on that morning. Lorenzo and I became fast friends within minutes. Shortly after meeting him, he was escorting me to class, with our mothers forgotten and walking far behind. We made it to class, found our seats and awaited the teacher's instructions.

Lorenzo and I were opposite in almost every way. He was confident, but I was fearful; he was outspoken; but I was quiet; he was smart and friendly, but I felt ignorant and was very introverted. I am convinced that the Lord placed this little boy in my life to keep me from severe emotional trauma. My mind was entrenched in a pool of fearfulness and paranoia of everything and anyone that I didn't know, including other kids. But, Lorenzo talked and played with me often, and with his help I made it through each day. Unfortunately, I didn't progress in any way with other students or with assigned activities, aside for the occasional coloring and finger painting task, in which I participated only with Lorenzo's prompting.

For me, first grade wasn't much different than the previous summer's Head Start program. I was a little less fearful going into the first grade, but that was because I knew Lorenzo would be there with me. In Mrs. Prince Brown's class, my first grade teacher, there were more students than were at summer school. For some reason this alarmed me. Upon reflection, I can see how potentially dangerous an effect fear could have had on my mental condition. Though I am not formally trained as a psychologist, I have for years and at different periods in my adult life observed youths who showed the same outward signs and patterns. For example, there was one particular adolescent boy, who exemplified, in some ways, what I may have become had God not intervened. Working as an instructional assistant in the special education department at Varina High School in Henrico County, Virginia., I worked in close proximity to children of various mental and/or emotional diagnoses. This youngster, with whom I worked daily, on a one-on-one basis, was very introverted, fearful of every one except his mother, and was extremely paranoid that someone was trying to hurt him or speak lies about him. Also, as a youth, I feared that other children would try to hurt me without reason or provocation. This young boy's problem was so severe that on one occasion his mother couldn't get him out of the car to step onto the school's grounds. The grip of fear had such a stronghold on him, such that, he feared for his life, though without cause. This condition made it difficult for him to concentrate on his studies, but rather spent much of his time surveying the class for possible movements toward him. He, as well as some others in the special education department, had to leave their classes before the school's bell rang, because of the fear of being in the presence of the student population. This grip of fear had interfered with his progress in academics, and in many other aspects of growth. Therefore this young boy was placed among the mildly to severely mentally challenged, thus being deleted from normal and fruitful opportunities that he may have had the abilities to accomplish. I am grateful to God for saving me from such an end, because, as is witnessed and sometimes quoted by enlightened believers, "but for the grace of God there goest I."

Progressing as best I could through the first grade, I was thankful that the Lord had placed Lorenzo in my path. Even at that age I sensed that God was intervening on my behalf. Yet, I was not prepared for what was to come, that is, the second grade. It had not occurred to me that school would change from year to year. I believed that there would be the same boys and girls with me forever. However, this was not the case. Upon entering the second grade classroom, again with Mrs. Brown as my teacher, I immediately noticed that there was no Lorenzo among us. This would not have disrupted my emotions so badly, thinking he may have been away from the room momentarily, but there were others missing also. Somehow I knew that he and the others would not be returning to our class. On that very first day in the second grade, I reverted back to that first day at Head Start. I began crying uncontrollably, and complaining of a severe stomachache. This extreme bellowing went on for much of the year. I would see my dear friend periodically on most days, such as at lunch and recess. Though, I could see that he had made new friends, he seemed to take a little time to talk with me from day to day; and I found this to be very encouraging. Lorenzo truly epitomized that which the Holy Bible states about the committed friendships. In Proverbs 18:24 it says *" A man that hath friends must shew himself friendly: and there is a friend that sticketh closer than a brother"*. Surely, Lorenzo was, and remains, like a brother to me; and I am truly grateful to him for his loyalty to our friendship.

Along with my reluctance to reach out to other children came a stigma that attached itself to me. I was labeled a cry-baby and a weakling. I was a prime target for any bully in the class, whether boy or girl. If someone looked at me with any negativity I would cry or isolate myself in my own little shell. It seems I was picked on much, never to take a stance against those who treated me badly. Even when I became angry and tired of the pushing, shoving, plucking and smacking in the back of my head, and the mean things that were sometimes said to me, the fear in my heart wouldn't be overridden by my instincts to address those who bullied me. Strangely enough, I wouldn't tell my teachers or parents. The students considered me as an out-right whimp. From the second through the fifth grades, I often faked being sick, fearful to go to school. Fortunately, reading with some degree of proficiency, I felt compelled to read the Bible. I read from the first chapter of Genesis every time I opened it. I felt myself being built up and shored up when reciting, *"In the beginning God created the heaven and the earth"* (Ge 1:1 *KJV*). I was convinced in my heart that these words were written for me. Somehow, I knew that God was in the midst of all that He had created, even me. I understood what the older saints meant when they said, "I know that I know that I know". Although they could not express it verbally, they had an assurance and an understanding from God that He was with them, and is their rock and their salvation. I knew, in my spirit, that this was also true for me. Just a few words from the scriptures, stirred up by the Holy Ghost, brought about breakthroughs in my life. By the leading of the Holy Spirit, I received psychotherapy in reading the Word of God, and prayer. The more I read, the more convinced I became that God was my protector and my shield from incoming attacks. I became confident in many areas of my life. Forging on with new friendships, I became more active and interested in athletics, and my focus on academics greatly improved. Most of all, my desire to know God, and His Word, grew dramatically. I began to see that as I studied and prayed, the greater my loosening from a spirit of fear. Again, in reflection, I see that God's Word did not return to Him void. It is written in James 4:7 " *Submit yourselves therefore to God. Resist the devil, and he will flee from you" (KJV).*

## Chapter 9

# The Non-Discerning of Influences

*Stumbling blocks and deceptions*

Sixth grade and turning twelve combined to foster an almost metamorphic like change in my persona. My physique was becoming more masculine and pronounced, and my voice and facial structure matured. Girls began showing interest in me, and secretly, I in them. Although hesitant, I was no longer reluctant to enter into the total scholastic experience.

That once shy crybaby was no longer present among his peers. I did not qualify as the big man on campus, but I was not to be the target of bully practice any more. My determination to be included as part of the student body was fixed, and I began to activate myself in every available activity that was allowed. I participated in classroom discourse, as well as extracurricular activities. Anxiously, I volunteered on every opportunity to be part of any school play or sports activity. The level of confidence I exhibited was rising in respect to conversing with girls and co-mingling with the more aggressive boys. Though I continued to have a sense of fear of my peers, my desire to overcome was stronger. Secretly, at night in my bedroom, I prayed and studied scripture. My faith in Christ, and in trusting what the Bible professed, was growing. Each day I reaffirmed in my heart that which Jesus said in his Word. Two of the most effective scriptures of which I remained mindful are found in the Gospels. In St. John 16:33 Jesus says, *"But take heart! I have overcome the world"*, *a*nd in St. Matthew 28:20 He states, *"...And surely I am with you always, to the very end of the age" (NIV)*. It seemed like there was fire and power being forged in my heart, even throughout my whole being, just as a blacksmith billows and stokes his fire to build it into fervent heat, so was my soul set afire with every thought of Jesus' words. I could most assuredly identify with the prophet Jeremiah when he said, *"But his word was in mine heart as a burning fire shut up in my bones"* (Jeremiah 20:9 KJV).

The sixth grade was an exciting time. I loved playing baseball and football with the other guys at recess and during physical education class. Most confident in basketball play, I developed a level of skill that allowed me to compete with a consistent degree of success (this is according to my estimation). Periodically, some of the better players would compliment me on my abilities. I would truly get pumped up when I was among the first to be chosen for teams. It is amazing how the influence that a child's peer has on his self-esteem. My mother consistently spoke encouraging words to my brothers and me, which did wonders for our outlook. However, when my peers spoke praises, it made me feel worthy of acceptance. It is written in Proverbs 27:17, *"Iron sharpeneth iron; so a man sharpeneth the countenance of his friend."* This positive influence helped me to see another's need who also displayed an introverted posture. I would sometimes befriend those who stood in the corners during free class time or played alone on the outside basketball court while their classmates played in the gym. On several occasions, I joined one particular white kid during recess on the outdoor basketball court, even in cold weather. Coincidentally, his name was David, and I felt very comfortable around him. The schools in Charles City County had recently integrated, and there was very little co-mingling among the black, white and Indian students. There was some social interaction, but it developed slowly and reluctantly. Nevertheless, David and I did not experience any personal barriers between us at school. I tried to get his phone number on several occasions, but he refused. He was not very clear on why this was such a problem, but from all indications, I sensed that his parents wouldn't want such a relationship for him. I felt that he feared I'd see him in a different light had I called his home and subjected myself to conversation with other than himself. As David and I were promoted to high school, which begin with seventh grade, he gradually, but I believe purposefully, loosed himself out of our friendship. David never professed that he had a propensity for bigotry toward blacks, but made mention that he was aware of it within his family. I feel, in my heart, that racist influences found within his family, maybe even his own household, fostered that severing of our friendship. On two occasions, more than fifteen years after our high school graduation, I saw David at a seven-eleven, located on Rt. 5, in the Varina District of Henrico County. I spoke to him, in a friendly way, on both occasions, but he made no response. Being only inches from him as he exited the door, it was obvious that he purposefully ignored me. Both times, the memory of indications that he was being reared amongst racists came flashing back to my mind. The time we spent together playing ball, studying for tests, talking about the issues of life (as seen through the eyes of a child), and the overall efforts we put into developing a binding friendship, came to naught. Somehow, through the irrational influences of taught hate, he became offended by what I was, and did not rely on his knowledge of who I was. Any attempts, that I may have made to restore our friendship, had I been given the opportunity, would have certainly been hard fought. It is stated in Proverbs 18:19 that *" A brother offended is harder to be won than a strong city: and their contentions are like the bars of a castle"*. I do not harbor any resentment toward David for his choice to recant our relationship. Nevertheless, I was hurt by his weak stance toward the loyalty of our friendship. A good friend should be as close as a brother.

About the time I entered high school, I began experimenting with drinking alcohol and marijuana. A cousin from out of town introduced me to the pleasures that could be found from imbibing and smoking reefer. The habit came unto me quite craftily. My cousin, who was very intelligent by any academic standard, and courteous in his deportment, became my role model. He had a positive effect on me as far as academics were concerned, and was positive as to the good things the future held for us. Yet, this was the way by which the deception and provocation to do drugs crept in.

By the time I entered into the seventh grade I had already heard the myths about certain drugs and the effects that abuse has on a person's life. We were formally told that marijuana was harmful to one's psyche. Smoking pot (another name for marijuana) would drive a person crazy. However, when I saw people using pot, there were no visible signs of mental illness (at least as far as I understood mental illness). I thought that the user would show immediate signs of mental retardation, or exhibit violent and psychotic behavior. Yet, I witnessed excessive laughter, some foolish banter, and for some, an increase in the use of profanity. The use of alcohol was always a mainstay in every pot party, which exacerbated the aforementioned effects. But, this did not seem to exemplify the kinds of dangerous symptoms that we thought manifested in users. I began to question the veracity of the warnings that came from academic sources, and gave ear to the testimonies of those who used drugs. We heard, from streetwise sources and pro-marijuana advocates, that pot was not addictive, not psychologically harmful, and were able to increase one's intelligence. Also, we were told that marijuana had positive medicinal uses, such as painkillers, appetite inducers for eating disorders, and possible benefits for cancer and glaucoma patients. My cousin convinced me that marijuana causes euphoria that one had never experienced before. He expressed that the "high" was pleasant, calming, peaceful, and fostered a happy feeling. Unbeknown to me, he was describing a kind of a religious experience. Years later I would find out some information about drug addiction that really blew my mind. I researched the spiritual aspects of drugs used in various cultures, from a historical and a biblical standpoint. In the mist of this research I found that the background for certain words used in our modern English language, relative to drugs, had very interesting and enlightening meanings. For example, the word pharmaceutical comes from the Greek word *"pharmakeia"*, and a maker of drugs, in the Greek is *"pharmakon"*. Pharmakeia, translated in the biblical English vernacular, means "sorcery" or "witchcraft", and pharmakon is translated as refering to "a spell giving potion", "druggist", or "poisoner" (this information was taken from THE NEW STRONG'S EXHAUSTIVE CONCORDANCE OF THE BIBLE). (I would like to note that the words expounded in this paragraph don't refer to medications prescribed by qualified doctors and filled by qualified pharmacists, but rather refer to modern day sorcerers, and doers of witchcraft, i.e.

Satan's pawns, heretofore known as "drug dealers". Also, those who were under the spells of the potions that were made by these drug dealing sorcerers and witches, are, nowadays, known as drug users and addicts).

As I grew older and began considering the issues of life, I depended on marijuana to help me envision what kind of life to pursue and the way by which I might accomplish my goals. Not realizing it at the time, I allowed marijuana to replace prayer and meditation. However, I embraced any opportunity to smoke pot, and used the high as an avenue to the fantasy zone. My pot smoking friends and I would drive about the county getting high, without any regard for our own safety or the safety of others. We, in our early days of drug use, had no fear of the possibility of being caught by the sheriff. It was as if we didn't know that the possession and use of marijuana was a criminal offense. As I increased my sphere of associations I realized how prevalent pot was in our county. Everywhere I went people were smoking. I smoked with uncles, cousins, friends, and acquaintances. I was surprised to see some who were normally quiet, respectful to teachers, cooperative, and studious, smoking pot. There were boys and girls, the popular and unpopular, the good and bad, the smart and academically slothful; teachers and students, all getting high, and sometimes in the same places at the same time. Places such as our county's community center, various house parties, a local dance club called the Phase IV Supper Club, were very popular gathering places for pot smoking. Also, several beer joints, sometimes called "beer gardens" or "juke joints", were daily get high spots, especially during the summer months. Please understand that these establishments did not formally sanction such activities on their premises. However, it was impossible for those in charge to not know that such happenings occurred. They turned their heads as to these occurrences, and all for the love of money. In a way, these alcohol-selling establishments, because of their knowledge of the mass use of marijuana on their premises, enabled addicts to abuse pot, and other drugs. This unspoken permission to use on the premises, whether indoors or out, produced more consumers for these places of business. This fact made the business owners as accountable for the proliferation of drugs as were the drug pushers. The managements knew what was going on, yet were conveniently silent, and profited from the fruit of the drug trade.

Although pot was immensely popular, I was not completely blind as to the negative effects of its use. I could see how marijuana gradually made my friends and me paranoid and lazy. I also found it harder to study with any comprehension. Years later, I experienced short-term memory loss and increased anxiety. However, I soon realized that my entire lifestyle changed with periods of abstinence. My grades improved, comprehension and retention increased, and I forged better friendships when abstaining from smoking. There was even a better and clearer understanding of the scriptures, as I read the Bible, than during attempts at studying the Word when using pot. I knew that I was losing ground with my relationship with Christ, but by this time, the addiction to pot, and later to other drugs, had taken root. No one I knew could put the ax to the root of this problem. The answer to the problem was in the Word of God, but I was not as spiritually discerning, nor did those around me know how to address this truly spiritual conflict. Therefore, the addiction grew to what eventually became a chronic and daily habit.

During my high school years, especially grades 9 thru 12, I increased extracurricular activities, such as sports, and took on a more challenging course load. I was very desirous for college, and to impress a wonderful girl named Cathy. This business fostered a decrease in my drug use. However, during the summer months, I relished the use of smoking pot as often as possible. This pattern during those years brought about even greater deception concerning the use of drugs, because I believed that doing drugs could be expedient if used at the right time, and even as a possible reward for accomplishing one's goals. If I had only known that which is written in Proverbs 16:25 which states, "There *is a way that seemeth right to a man, but the end thereof are the ways of death"*. *(KJV)*

It would be many years later before I'd find Proverbs 16:25, and several close calls with death, due to drug related activity, but, even during those high school years, I experienced a spiritual demise in my life with every puff. Also, the more I sensed the wrong of it, the more I felt a lack of closeness to God. As I voluntarily subjected myself to getting high and drinking alcohol, I sensed a moving away from the Lord, as well as from my family and Cathy. I felt a desperate need to stop using, yet was powerless to do so. I rationalized that the drug use would eventually extinguish itself. But I knew in the back of my mind that it would not leave, and was an ungodly and unfruitful presence in my life that pitched a stronghold in my being. I sensed this marijuana addiction was a spirit of some sort, though I could not articulate what I felt. I sensed that it had attached itself to my flesh, or rather my fleshly mind. My need for fleshly pleasures and euphoria struggled with that part of my being that remained desirous of the presence of God. This testifies of a truth expressed by Paul in his letter to the Galatians 5:17 which says, " *For the flesh lusteth against the Spirit, and the Spirit against the flesh: and these are contrary the one to the other..."(KJV)*

## Chapter 10

# Boys Will Be Boys, Men Will Be Men

*The deception of false teachings upon the youth via accepted traditional sayings, and societal influences*

The desire for sexual experience had been sown in me since age six, as mentioned in earlier chapters. This belief was edified by the influences I came in contact with among older relatives and schoolmates, as well as my own hormonal desires. The issue of resisting fornication was never taught to me, or even spoken of in my adolescence. Smoking pot was a persistent pursuit, but wanting to have sex was a constant, and mind conspiring past-time; especially as I pursued my newly acquired girlfriend, Cathy. I liked that she was sort of shy and slightly introverted. I didn't like it when girls were loud and boisterous. Also, she was smart, pretty, nice, and physically mature. I felt it an honor to be her boyfriend. However, *my* perspective of so-called honorable intentions were wrong, and I falsely believed that my pursuit of her in our high school relationship, sexually speaking, was equally desirous by her.

I had known of Cathy since the sixth grade. Although she didn't know who I was, I watched her from afar on the playground during recess. She seemed to have plenty of friends, and was very playful. She even had more physical maturity than her female peers. I believe that is the first thing that caught my interest about her. However, I found her to be also pretty, yet, aloof. This infatuation from afar lasted up to high school. Until then, I had no classes with her. Then, in September 1973, the eighth grade, we were put in the same pre-algebra class. I was very excited. I discovered that Cathy was intelligent and friendly, and this blew my mind even more. I found myself competing with her, and other popular students, for greater academic success. Also I wanted to get Cathy's attention, for she had not a clue as to who I was. Nevertheless, I found out some things about myself. I discovered that I could do well academically. With a lot of studying, and classroom participation, I grasped the difficult concepts of the natural sciences. I truly enjoyed learning, and felt more self-esteem because of my increase in academic stature. This made me less reluctant to speak in front of others, especially among the more popular students. I believed I was no longer perceived as "dumb", and was less likely to say something immature. However, in the minds of the girls in that algebra class, most of us boys, regardless of our academic prowess, were stupid and immature. Oftentimes we opened our mouths and proved them right. I believe that we all had the same life's concerns, which included our short-and long-term future plans, friendships, intimate relationships, sports activities, and college considerations. We were studious and diligent in our studies. Becoming friends, we increased our level of academic competition among each other, and edified one another in our level of comprehension and success. Although mentioned in a previous chapter, Proverbs 27:17 bears repeating, in that, *"As Iron sharpeneth iron; so a man sharpeneth the countenance of his friend"*.

My fixation with Cathy remained relatively strong, although, during the 9th and 10th grades I experienced other relationships, but they were brief and minor. It was during February '76 that I gained the courage to address Cathy as to my feelings about her. We were traveling to an away basketball game. I played Junior varsity, and she was on the cheering squad. Somehow, while on the bus, a group of us entered into a conversation about couples being committed to each other. Cathy had expressed a commitment to her present boyfriend, and swore her dedication. At that point in time, I went for broke. Not knowing how to approach the issue, I stumbled into the conversation, saying that I could "swoon" her away. She counted my speaking as being foolish and ignorant. But, I was allowed to speak uninterrupted. I continued by saying that I had been watching her from afar, and thought she was among the better-looking girls in our class. I expressed my unyielding intentions to pursue, and that I would eventually woo her. Cathy said that she thought that I was "loony tunes", and a "foo fong". (I never did find out what was a "foo fong".)

It was about one month later, on our way to a track meet, that Cathy exemplified her desire to consider me as a possible boyfriend. We both were on the track team. I boldly sat beside her on the bus, and, to my surprise, she said nothing to indicate opposition. We both sat strangely quiet. Her friend, Jeri, approached me, and demanded that I get up and go to another seat. Before I could move or flinch, Cathy rebuked her and told her to move on. I was very pleased, but stunned and speechless. It was on that very day, March 16, 1976, that Cathy and I became an item. Although happy about this new relationship, I was inwardly confused, and filled with a lot of "stinking thinking" as to how relationships were supposed to develop. Unbeknown to either of us, this was the beginning of twenty years of an on again, off again tumultuous relationship.

The root of my problem was not seeing, with any consistency, that there *must* be a connection between my spiritual life and my social life. Thus, it was easy for me to violate my Christian responsibility in my relationship with Cathy. I was blind as to the need to regulate all social and personal associations by the precepts set out in the Word of God. While desiring to know Jesus more personally, and wanting to fill my appetite for the Word, I didn't know that I was to acknowledge God in all my ways, as mentioned in Proverbs 3:6. Just as many professed Christians falsely believe that there should be a separation between church and state, for the Bible doesn't say that such a notion is acceptable, nor is the first amendment correctly interpreted when it is said that the constitution upholds such a notion. Similarly, I also believed that there was a separation between my personal relationship with Christ and my relationship with Cathy, as well as in my relationship with others who periodically shared their drugs with me. However, I must confess that I sensed, especially *after* I committed transgressions, a separation from God. It was a feeling that is similar to what I perceived as a dying experience. But these feelings of grief would soon pass, and again I focused on the flesh, and ignored the unction of the Spirit.

While struggling between the things of the flesh and the things of the spirit during my tenth grade year, I was asked to be the assistant superintendent of my church's Sunday school. Though privately reluctant, I accepted. Upon reflection, God was showing me a way of escape from the tribulations that were to come, fostered by my lack of judgment.

My relationship with Cathy began to spin out of control early on. I wanted to kiss her all the time, and demanded a lot of attention. She didn't say much as to her discomfort with my pursuit, but I sensed that she was highly uncomfortable with the way I tried to develop our relationship. I felt that we had to be separate from everyone, that is, only talk to one another, and ignore our friends. I was ignorant as to how to began a worthy relationship. Cathy was more mature, and was better able to regulate our friendship, but I was very aggressive, and forged ahead as I thought my peers expected. This is not to say that all of our peers lacked knowledge of God's morality, for some were very astute as to sexual morality, and as far as I knew, they walked in their knowledge of the truth. But, I was more influenced by those boys that believed one should seek to verify their relationship by having sex. This influence came mainly through associations with the party and pot smoking crowd. Oh! How foolish I was at that pivotal time in my life. Though mindful of that which the Bible says about the types of associations we ought to have, I, through the lust of the flesh, decided to act contrary to what the scriptures say in Psalms 1:1-2, *"(1) Blessed is the man that walketh **not** in the counsel of the ungodly, **nor** standeth in the way of sinners, **nor** sitteth in the seat of the scornful. (2) But his **delight** is in the law of the Lord; and in **his law** doth he **meditate day and night.**"(KJV)*

My energies were used in bringing about situations whereby I could dilute Cathy's resistance to abstinence from sex. I always wanted her alone to myself, to separate her from friends and classmates, whether we were at school, a dance, or after a ball game. I did not realize it then, but I was conspiring to bring about a "curse" on her life, by convincing her to forsake the law of the Lord in regards to sex outside of marriage. By my relentless pursuit, I was inadvertently teaching her to do that which the Bible says is sin, that is, to commit fornication.

Eventually, in mid October 1976, I convinced a highly reluctant and very nervous Cathy to allow me to touch her in that forbidden way. This was accomplished by weeks of periodic kissing and heavy petting, which I swore would never escalate into anything more. I deceived her, but was unaware that the lust of my flesh, coupled with the circumstances fostered by temptations, would eventually lead to her becoming weak in her conviction to resist sexual intimacy.

Although we did transgress the commandment of God, He did send us warnings to not fall into this temptation. First of all, he sent his Word to come into our hearing. I studied at Sunday school, while assistant superintendent, in Mrs. Lois Curl's class, who had also been my sixth grade school teacher, that succumbing to youthful lust was dangerous and sinful. Cathy had also confessed that she felt that our petting and excessive kissing was not acceptable to the Lord, and much more so, actual sexual intercourse. Yet, we gave our flesh greater reign over our relationship than to the Holy Spirit.

Another spiritual warning, manifested in this realm of reality, came our way. I believe it was in September 1976 that we found ourselves in Byrd Park, located in Richmond Virginia. We were in a clearing area, near a small pond, and lying under a big oak tree. Kissing on a blanket, we were approached by two strangers. Standing before us were men, as I remember, arrayed in hooded robes. We could not see their faces clearly. They appeared to be young men, in their early twenties. One was a black man, the other white. As, they approached us, I remember seeing that each of them carried a book. The black gentleman carried a very large book; approximately six inches thick, whereas the other had a smaller book, about the size of a normal size soft back King James Bible. One of them spoke to us and said, "Do you know what you do?" I replied, "What is it that you want?" The other man spoke and said, "Will you let us tell you some things about what you're doing?" I became offended and expressed my anger. I rebuked them for interrupting our privacy, and discourteously told them to leave us alone. Once more they beseeched us to allow them to speak. I again responded with my previous admonishment. In the meantime, Cathy remained silent and fixated on them during the entire conversation. The two looked saddened, turned and walked away. I immediately looked at Cathy to see if she had an expression of astonished offense, as did I. But, the strangest thing happened at that point in time. While the two men walked away in the same direction from which they came, after I turned to look at Cathy's face, which took an estimated two seconds, I turned again to watch the men leave, but they were no longer in the clearing beyond. There was only spacious area between the tree that we sat under and the entire circumference of the area. There is no way those men could have left our sight in a matter of seconds, even if they ran. There had to be at least seventy yards between us and the next set of geographical obstructions in the direction in which those men walked. Upon reflection of this incident, those men simply disappeared! It wasn't until about fifteen years later that Cathy and I came to the possible conclusion that these men may have been angels. In my mind I thought that this may be a far-fetched explanation, until I studied, in the Word of God, that God has given his holy angels charge over us, which is confirmed in Psalm 34:7 and in Psalm 91:11. Also, the Word of God explains that He allows his angels to minister to us, as it is written, in respect to the Lord's angels, in the epistle to the Hebrews 1:14, " *Are they not all ministering spirits, sent forth to minister for them who shall be heirs of salvation?"(KJV)* Furthermore the Bible says in Hebrews 13:1-2, in respect to angels appearing in human form, presenting themselves before men, *"(1) Let brotherly love continue. (2) Be not forgetful to entertain strangers: for thereby some have entertained angels unawares"*. This is quite an awesome thought, that God, in His omniscience, dispatched angels to minister to Cathy and me. Though we didn't receive His efforts to warn us of the tribulations that were to come our way due, God saw afar off, and knew that we would one day love and desire Him with all our heart. Thus, He knew that Cathy and I would remember our experience, witness of it to others who would experience similar relational dysfunction, and compel them to surrender to God. AMEN!

## Chapter 11

# From Friend
# to Foe

*A [girlfriend] offended is harder to win*
*than a strong city, and their contentions*
*are like the bars of a castle.*

At age sixteen, I was not aware of the possible relational problems that can occur in an intimate relationship. My knowledge was basically limited to thinking that a high school affair consisted of kissing, holding hands, talking on the phone at every and any possible hour, and looking at each other with "goo-goo" eyes. However, Cathy was more mature in conversation than I. She talked about romance and the need to show affection in non-physical ways, such as, surprising one another with flowers, writing poetry, taking walks, and talking about the Lord's will for our lives. I was convinced of her notions of expressing other forms of affection. Also, to some extent, I tried to do those things. I especially liked it when she initiated conversations about the Lord. We could talk about many things that we pondered in our hearts relative to our walk with Christ. We were in agreement, even at that stage of our lives, with the Word of God, and we were made glad by it. However, though in verbal and mental agreement, we were not in "doing agreement" with His Word. The Bible states in James 1: 22, "But *be ye doers of the word, and not hearers only, deceiving your own selves*". (*KJV*) Cathy and I were deceived as to our receiving any favor and blessing that we believed may come from the Lord, not realizing, more perfectly, that rewards are connected to our posture of humility toward the will of God to walk in obedience to his word. This truth is revealed to us in Hebrews 11:6, "...*for he that cometh to God must believe that he is, and that he is a rewarder of them that diligently seek him*". Our problem was not that we were not receiving the knowledge of the Word of God, but that we were not *walking* in our knowledge of the truth. Our lack of obedience to God's word hindered our maturity in our relationship with him and with one another. We confessed to one another that we sensed a compelling to submit ourselves to Christ's commandments, yet did not. This unction that we felt was an urging from the Holy Spirit, of which, we, by my own rebellious insistence, walked in disobedience, thus, dramatically hindering our spiritual maturity. In the book The Bait of Satan, written by John Bevere, he states, in chapter six, entitled " HIDING FROM REALITY", that " Physical growth is a function of time...Intellectual growth is a function of learning. Spiritual growth is neither a function of time or learning, but it is a function of obedience...Even though we continue to learn, we never mature because of disobedience".

My own desire to act contrary to God's unction sowed the seeds of dysfunction in Cathy's and my relationship shortly after we came together. When it became known that Cathy and I were romantically involved, there were some of my peers that urged me to not continue in that relationship. Their reasons for suggesting our breakup were not founded in any truth, but in lying rumors, and in some cases, feminine conspiracies to woo my interest elsewhere. However, I was not convinced as to those reasons. But, through a constant bombardment by others admonishing me to break up with her, I began to weaken. Cathy had given me a metal bracelet to symbolize our commitment. Carved into it were the words "I Love you". I knew that she felt in her heart that very thing. One day after school, during track practice, I gave into the pressure and cowardly asked my friend, Tyree, to give the bracelet back to Cathy. We were in the gym at this time, and she was involved in a cheering squad activity. I could see the look on her face as Tyree gave her that bracelet and told her I was breaking up with her. At first, the sight of her hurtful expressions, which I witnessed from the extreme opposite of the gym, gave me a brief sense of power, but, as I exited the gym, descending the steps entering into G-building, which housed the school's library, I sensed a feeling of grief in my spirit, that is, a kind of a dying within myself. I, again, negatively had affected my relationship with Christ. I had grieved the Holy Spirit, not realizing that Cathy was a child of God. I had insensitively violated Jesus' commandment to be kind to one another, and love one another. But, that which I had done was cruel, weak-hearted, and insensitive. I remember feeling weak all over, sensing that something left me at that moment. I wonder if King David of the Bible felt that way when he beseeched the lord in Psalm 51: 11, saying, " *Cast me not away from thy presence; and take not thy holy spirit from me*". *(KJV)* I sensed a need to repent, though I didn't know, at that time, that technically that was what I was feeling. Soon after, I did repent of what I had done. The Bible teaches that we are to be quick to repent. So, I apologized fervently to her. However, I knew that she harbored the hurt that she had just experienced. I began to notice, within that same day, that Cathy changed slightly. She began to be slower in her affectionate expressions, and began to speak often on whatever character defects that she saw in me. For the first time in my life I felt what it was like to be spurned by someone for whom you had professed a heart-felt affection. As time went on, so did our back and forth antics that promoted broken-heartedness in one another.

During this period in our relationship, Cathy began feeling ambivalent toward me. I noticed that some days she showed much interest in me as a boyfriend, while other days she was standoffish. She would seem to flirt with other boys, which resulted in me being very jealous. I never thought that she would actually leave me for them, but I didn't know how to rationalize her spurning me in this way with any degree of maturity. I would call her on the phone and discuss my disapproval with her talking with other boys, even though I sensed it was innocent. I knew Cathy wanted to continue in our relationship, but she was unsure about my loyalty. Thus, she tried on the one hand to create an atmosphere that she lightly esteemed our relationship, while on the other hand, when talking on the phone, she related to me with all earnestness that she wanted our relationship to work. Some days she would speak to me as if she didn't want to continue seeing me romantically, while on other days Cathy would shower me with words of affection. I felt like a "yo-yo". Yet, I sensed that she wanted to protect herself from any possible hurt that may come, as had happened with the bracelet incident.

In October of 1976, I pursued an act that changed every plan of our personal futures. The intent of my heart was to have sexual relations with Cathy, and I pursued that tenaciously. Although I had a heated desire to enter into a sexual affair, yet, due to a lack of experience, I had no laid out plan. However, the impulse to say and do certain things, while Cathy was very vulnerable, was successful in leading to a sexual engagement. The inspiration *was not* inspired by God. So, the question is who or what was the inspiring entity that aided me in accomplishing the lust that I harbored in my heart? I would venture to say that it was the tempter/enticer, that is, Satan or one of his cohorts. After all, the Bible says that Satan is the prince of the devils. Therefore, we can infer that Satan can assign his demons to attack and provoke both believers and unbelievers so to compel their thinking toward ideas that they normally would not consider. The Bible shows that Satan can interject his thoughts into our mind. Satan is the tempter, and we know that he often tried to influence the thinking processes of even chosen men of God. Jesus himself was tempted three times by Satan after the Holy Spirit led him into the wilderness, after he fasted forty days and was of extreme hunger (Matthew 4: 1-10). The Bible also teaches that Satan influenced the apostle Peter's thinking on several occasions. For example, in the gospel of St. Matthew 16: 22-23, Jesus rebukes Satan for provoking Peter to speak rebukingly to Him. Jesus says to Peter in verse 23, after turning to him to respond to the rebuking comment that he made concerning the prophesy of Jesus' impending death, *"Get thee behind me, Satan: thou art an offence to me: for thou savourest not the things that be of God, but those things that be of men"*.

I didn't understand the actual activity that went into play in giving into lust, especially the attack that ensues from spirits of darkness, which are assigned to make believers deny their faith. It is written in the scriptures in James 1:14, *"But every man is tempted, when he is **drawn away** of his own lust, and **enticed"***.

With every opportunity to make Cathy feel insecure about our relationship, for she wanted so very much to keep it going, I was inspired to manipulate her to fear our breakup. I showed outward interest in other girls, spoke to her in a disappointing fashion in regard to our lack of physical intimacy; made her believe that I respected her decision not to have sex; was thankful for the petting she allowed (though that was part of the process that led to intercourse), yet, I needed more. Somehow I knew that since I had been successful in getting Cathy to commit her heart, due to fear of losing me, which was evidenced by the petting that she eventually allowed, and the realization that she lacked self esteem when it came to maintaining personal relationships, and continual pursuit, I would see the lust of my flesh fulfilled.

One day, during mid October 1976, I asked Cathy to visit me. I was inspired to give her the impression that I had some sad news concerning our relationship (this inspiration was not from God). Although I didn't speak it, but inferred that I wanted to break up with her, but face to face. Upon reflection, I believed that on that day I knew that Cathy would give in to my pursuit of sexual intercourse. Interestingly, I sensed that Cathy felt all her procrastination was ended, and she had to choose whether to keep or let me go. So, I began so see that her *fear* of losing me would take over where I left off. Consequently, she and her sister Crystal came to visit our home. Cathy asked her sister to stay at my house for a few minutes while we took a drive. There was very little talking between us as we went to a private place, and with no words spoken, we entered into that forbidden act. After it was over, Cathy began to weep. I ached at the look of sadness on her face. As for me, I felt a sense of fear that I couldn't articulate. I believe that both of us were horrified by what had just happened. Somehow, Cathy and I knew that she would become pregnant from this very first time, and she did.

This happened on a Saturday afternoon. On the following Monday, at school, we said nothing to one another. I really don't remember when we talked again after that eventful Saturday, but eventually we did talk. Cathy's first words to me were, "I hate you! You bastard!" For months, she only spoke similar words. She went the remaining of our eleventh grade term in abject disgust of me. There was a time that we were so close, but now, friendship turned into hate. I did seek forgiveness from God and Cathy, but I sensed a separation from God, probably due to my lack of knowledge to come to *Godly* repentance. Though sincerely sorry for what was done, and for Cathy's horrifying predicament, I was not truly committed to turning away from that sin. Thus, I found no peace in my confession to God, or of negatively affecting another person's life. Furthermore, I did not make a stance to take responsibility for the consequences of my actions. I left Cathy to face the pregnancy alone. The remaining of that school year Cathy and I sunk into a serious depression, not confiding in anyone, nor facing the truth of what was happening to her. We alienated ourselves from each other and every one around us, but mostly, in regard to her and myself, she was filled with an obvious and fervent hate, and expressed it with all ferocity. It amazed me how quick a person's disposition can change, but, it is written in Proverbs 18:19, " A brother *(sister)* offended is harder to be won than a strong city: and their contentions are like the bars of a castle" *(italicized words and parenthesis added)KJV.*

As for me, I was too fearful to tell my parents or friends about the pregnancy. My parents heard, through a relative, that Cathy was with child. They received this news only one day before she had the baby—born July 21, 1977. On the very next day, I received a call, while working at the Charles City Community Center, as a swimming instructor, that Cathy had given birth to a boy. I panicked at the reality of this, not considering the thump of reality that Cathy must have felt. Prior to my mother's call, in a feeble attempt to anesthetize the sting of this certainty, I'd been drinking alcohol, heavily smoking reefer, and was totally blitzed! Somehow I gained the courage to go home where my mother ushered me into the shower. After which I hastily dressed and left for the hospital. My mother handled this with calm, and a purpose to support and encourage Cathy. Cathy named our son Jeffrey Dupree; and he has grown to be a devoted son to his mother and his siblings, who followed some fifteen years later.

## Chapter 12

# Taking the Agony With the Ecstasy— Emotionally Binding

*Relational dysfunction will be the result
of forbidden sexual activity*

We had tasted the fruit of sexual gratification, and, without true repentance from the first act of fornication, we fell for deception that suggested that once we had committed this forbidden act, we might as well continue in it. The thought that I had entered into the spiritual crime of sexual sin made me feel unworthy to live holy before the Lord. Now, my thinking became ambivalent, and confused. However, we know, according to 1Corithians 14:33, that "...God is not the author of confusion". Also, I was not mindful of God's promise, that is, if we confess our sins, God is "faithful and just to forgive us our sins and to cleanse us from all unrighteousness" — 1 John 1:9. I was not knowledgeable enough of God's truths at that time in my walk; thus, I bounced back and forth in my mindset in regard to understanding what I *really* was in Christ. I felt limited in the degree to which I followed Him. Since committing this sexual act, I thought that I had nullified any chance of God using me for His Kingdom. Thus, I falsely believed that continuing the pursuit of sexual gratification was merely a cause in the discontinuance of spiritual ambition, not a source that would lead to divine judgment. Also, in the back of my mind, I sensed that God was unctioning me to fight against the desires of my flesh, enter into His forgiveness with a commitment to follow his commandments, and to swim in the pool of his omnipresent Spirit. God wanted to fellowship with me, and I sensed it, but, due to my lack of consistent prayer and study, I resisted the Holy Spirit from confirming in my spirit that which he unctioned me to do. Consequently, my life in those days was filled with confusion, shame, and dysfunction.

When I entered into the arena of sexual activity, I unknowingly made several bonds with the one whom I copulated. Copulation is the joining of two people by way of sexual intercourse. Sexual activity is physical activity that has spiritual and emotional ramifications. God specifically sanctioned that it be reserved for marriage, so that the husband and wife could enter into an oneness in their lifelong relationship; and that they would be "fruitful and multiply". It is written in Ephesians 5:31, *"For this cause shall a man leave his father and mother, and shall be joined unto his wife, and they two shall be one flesh" (KJV).* Two people, in physical actuality, do not become meshed into one physical body (except in a temporary sense, during actual intercourse), therefore this verse refers to a spiritual oneness. Ideally, in accordance with the Word of God, they are one flesh living in symbolic oneness with one another, sharing in all things, in agreement with one another and Christ, as becometh saints. However, since the act of copulation can result in the procreation of a new soul, then this sexual act carries a spiritual component that results from and requires two people's participation. God has given human beings the power to procreate souls, which, consequently, will never die, spiritually. The Bible explains that whatever is born of the flesh is indeed flesh, as spoken by Jesus in the Gospel of St. John 3:6 (KJV). Thus, since the make up of a person involves a physical body and an invisible soul, then both are components of the creation of a person. Furthermore, our spiritual body, which is that part of the human makeup that is in God's image, for God is a spirit (St. John 4:24), is the catalyst whereby God ordains the quickening of our mortal flesh. This spiritual body also allows us to have the capacity to become one with Him, through Christ, and to know the "born again of the Holy Spirit" experience. (Note: read the Gospel of St. John 3: 3-8). So, the bonding that takes place during sexual intercourse is not only physical, but also spiritual, which is confirmed by the fact that the child produced is both flesh and soul. It is written in Malachi 2:15, in regards to married couples, "Has *not the Lord made them one? In flesh and spirit they are his. And why one? Because he was seeking godly offspring..." (NIV).* Thus, it follows that the sexual act fosters a physical bond and a soul bond, and these bondings produce fruit that is manifested as offspring (children), who are made alive by the Spirit of God, who plants another body into each person, that is, a spiritual body. For the Bible indicates that when a person dies, he leaves this realm of reality, the physical body decays, his soul sleeps until Christ's judgment via the rapture, or the second resurrection; and his spirit goes back to the Lord. It is written, by the apostle Paul, in 2 Corinthians 5:8, " *We are confident, I say, and willing rather to be absent from the body, and to be present with the Lord" (KJV).* Moreover, while our Lord and Savior hung on the cross, and said unto the Lord, as He gave up the Ghost (i.e. His divine Spirit which abided in His earthen vessel, for he was also a "son of man", as well as "the Son of God"), *"Father, into thy hands I commend my spirit".* Also, the Martyred disciple Stephen, being stoned to death for his witnessing of Christ, stated in Acts 7:59, *"...Lord Jesus, receive my __spirit__" (KJV).* In that same chapter of Acts, verse 60, it is said of Stephen that, "...when he had said this, he fell asleep", meaning, his soul fell asleep, that is, he died. Each part of a human being's make up has an immediate and different destination upon bodily death, with their soul being reserved until their respective Judgment resurrection.

Now that I have attempted to bring some clarity as to the physical and spiritual ramification of sexual bonding, I will reflect on the emotional ramification of this act of lust. The sin of committing fornication, results in that bonding act not being blessed of God, for we know that outside of holy matrimony, sexual activity is sin; and according to the apostle Paul it is even idol worship. Thus, not being blessed of God only results in relational and emotional dysfunction, regardless of one being a believer in Christ.

Dysfunction plagued my relationship with Cathy for many years. We both fell into the stronghold of fleshly lust; not knowing that a soul bond had developed, which stunted us emotionally. Moreover, our spiritual immaturity edified this stronghold. We could never find peace in our relationship, but only momentary gratification. Immediately after the sexual act came contentions, hurt, guilt, and further distancing from God. Though I could not see clearly the reasons for the contentions in our relationship, resulting from our illicit intimacies, I did sense that my chances to share true intimacy with Christ were becoming more aloof with every occasion in which I gave in to temptation.

Our relationship, that is, Cathy and mine's, was like a season in hell.

It was as though Cathy hated me, with a vengeance in her heart, yet couldn't let me go. Moreover, I loved her, i.e. mentally and emotionally, but not spiritually and dutifully, and could not hold on. Our lives, inside and out, were in disarray.

Going to school reluctantly, and periodically missing many days during my senior year, due to the shame of what I had done, I found peace in walking home from school. As stated in previous chapters, I went through periods where I sensed a strong unction to read God's Word, especially the Gospels. I would read for long periods of time, even several nights straight, over a period of weeks. I would stop, but again that same unction came over me. I found that the Word of God was compelling, embraceable, and empowering. Inwardly, I was filled with joy as I went through periods of study and meditation. Although I didn't understand at that time, my joy was caught up with the knowledge of God's Word. There was in me a strong desire to fellowship with the Lord, by meditating on His Word, and entertaining visions of my future as a fervent believer in Christ.

It was mysterious how this magnificent yearning to praise God, at this time in my life, with no one else present, was an overwhelming unction to me. So overwhelming, such that, I temporarily lost fear of things, though I had not overcome them permanently. A particular case in point is when I would decide to walk home, just to be alone with God in my meditations and reflections on His Word. This was mysterious because I was very fearful of walking home from school, especially alone. There was little more than a half-mile distance from my old high school, in the Ruthville area of our county, to my home. A length of distance in the rural country appears longer than in a more populated city area, so the trek from school to home was perceived, in my mind, as fatiguing, especially after football or track practice. But the reason for my fearfulness was the neighborhood dogs. As a young child, our next-door neighbor's dog viciously attacked me. They actually had two malicious dogs, with one being more vicious than the other. My brother, Ricky, and I had the task of fetching water from our neighbor's outdoor pump-house. Periodically, the dogs, which were restrained by chains, broke loose. This seemed to happen, coincidentally, when it was my turn to get the buckets of water. It also happened with my brother Ricky on occasion, yet he seemed to have little fear of dogs. Usually we were able to outrun the less vicious of the two, for he was the one that usually broke loose. But he would not venture into our yard, which was separated by a half-acre of bushes from our neighbor's, with a very thin path laid in the middle, connecting the two yards. (I must say that this was good training for our track future, as well as with other sports activities in which we participated.) But on one particular day the most vicious broke his chain. He chased me all the way to my doorstep and caught me there. He attacked me with all ferocity. Thankfully, our dog, Rattler (also called King), was asleep under the house, and was awakened by the attack. Our dog, being the biggest and strongest, came to my rescue, fought, and chased him away. Actually, this was the second time that I had been attacked by this same dog, as well as being attacked by the other dog, though less viciously. This explains the source of my fear of dogs.

My walk from school was also laden with dogs at several homes on the way. These animals were not restrained. As a younger boy, I walked with some of my older cousins along the road on our way home from the county's community center. Sometimes they strode a ways ahead of me or would make a detour while I, per my parent's instruction, had to come directly home. It was scary when the dogs would come to the edge of the road, with all their barking, growling, and posturing in the attack position. Being restrained by the number of us walking together, with sticks and rocks, they would rarely come within arms reach, but rather retreat at the swing of a stick or throw of a sizable rock. But when I found myself alone, I would be extremely long in building up the courage to pass each house that harbored a vicious dog, whether it was chained or loose. I remember obtaining the biggest, yet most handy piece of tree limb that I could find. I prayed with all fervency for as long as it took to build up courage and to be persuaded that God would protect me from harm. However, the best encouraging tool was the peace that came into my soul which persuaded me that if I were killed, I would appear in heaven with Christ. With that, I would proceed ahead and make the junket home. I was not mindful of this spiritual truth at the time, but I would do that which is admonished from the Word of God, that is, we are to persevere by building up our *"most holy faith"* (Jude 20th verse).

In those dog trials, I would overcome, out of necessity, by building up courage from God. But the fear of dogs remained in me, even through adolescence and early adulthood. Yet the fear of dogs withdrew during those high school years, whenever I became overwhelmed with the desire to be alone in my meditations, seasoned with thoughts of Christ, remembering the promises that He spoke in the Gospels. Particularly, that He would be with me always, even until the end of the world (Matthew 28:20).

I would get so caught up in fellowship, while on that walk home, that I sensed myself taking flight, spiritually, to another time. I could see myself speaking, with all excitement and with depth of truth, the Word of God, while sensing a great joy in my heart, which stoked that fire in me. I found myself experiencing that joy and fire while walking home during those many unstable days, catching myself speaking with excitement the truth of God's Word, reciting that which I had recently remembered from my Bible. I ministered the Word of God to myself, before the Lord. I sensed a great burden to let it flow out of me, as a rushing river. For the Word of God stirred me in a way that my feeble attempt at describing would not do it justice. Somehow I intuitively knew that Jesus wanted, at the point of this explosion in my spirit, to embrace me, love me, and abide in me permanently. God, by His grace, would, in those days, allow me to experience *His* joy and the *fire* of *His* Spirit. Even now, I cannot completely explain why the Lord allowed me this time with Him. However, I know that God can see afar off; and, as it is written in His Word, those that " he did foreknow, he also did predestinate...Moreover whom he did predestinate, them he also called"(Romans 8:29, 30). However, I also sensed a warning that I was as susceptible to the righteous judgments of God as I was His blessing. I knew that the posture that God would have toward me would depend upon the posture of obedience I had toward Him. Regrettably, I would so often allow the lust of the flesh and the entanglements of this world impede that which God, through his grace, allowed me to experience on the road to home.

## Chapter 13

# The Development of a Life Style

*A pattern of behavior fostered by the stronghold of lust and mind-altering substances*

During my senior year of high school, I entered into behavior patterns that would dictate the direction of my life's course. Though I tried to hold on to normal activities that were school, church, or community related, I fell into secret activities that were not known to anyone in my peer group or family, except the one family member with whom I participated in these secret gatherings. These gatherings were not secret per se, but were not known by my family and friends in Charles City. I participated in what amounted to a weekend pot smoking fest. At times, this involved alcohol, but mostly persistent reefer smoking.

This particular pattern of behavior began when my older cousin would pick me up on Friday nights to party with him and his friends. They attended Virginia Union University in nearby Richmond, Virginia. My cousin and I were good friends, so we shared a lot of activities. He introduced me to many of his fraternity buddies and other college friends, making me feel grown-up and independent. But, the introduction to his friends and college activities, both legitimate and illegal, were always brief. We, and occasionally his roommate, always returned to his dorm room smoking, and sometimes drinking, for hours upon hours, non-stop. Our reefer party was always accompanied with music that seemed to enhance the high we experienced. We inundated our hearing with music by such groups as Parliament and the Funkadelics, while becoming entranced by the stories that were told in the music, and the comic book stories published in the albums. Their music, in my experience, inspired hallucinating-like effects, (i.e. we were tripping!).

In great anticipation, I went from being picked up on weekends, to driving myself. Because my cousin was well mannered toward everyone, greatly liked, intelligent, and academically successful, my parents didn't mind that I spent excessive weekend time with him. In fact, they believed it was good for me to spend time around him instead of some of the neighborhood boys that seemed to have little ambition. My cousin did consistently emphasize the need for higher education in order to increase our chances for great financial and social success. However, I believed that getting high was a welcomed addition to the processes of achieving my goals. My cousin showed me that he was getting consistent A's, even in advanced studies, without sacrificing his "get-high" time. IT WAS ALL-GOOD! YEAH! So I thought. Oh! How much more foolish could I have been?

My cousin and I talked about God, but never discussed what might be the Lord's perspective about our pot smoking, for now our use had become chronic. I reminded myself that marijuana was not addictive, supposedly. Thus, using reefer was not inherently sinful. So, I resisted considering the possibility that my actions would negatively affect my relationship with God. Unknowingly, I was in denial.

My cousin and I had sown the seeds of this pattern of behavior during the summer after the completion of my tenth grade year and after I received my driver's license, June 1976. During this time, we secured jobs at the Sears and Roebuck store on West Broad St., near Virginia Union University. This store closed a few years after. We traveled to work in a used Yellowish Vega, and got high every day as we drove to and fro. My main purpose of wanting to work at Sears was so that I could share his pot. At that time I didn't have drug connections, money, nor knowledge of the in's and out's of buying on the "black market". I'd even lied about my age on the employment application for Sears, and told them that I was a freshman at VUU; they didn't verify age information in those days. That whole summer I was in a mental fog. It seemed that the only time I wasn't high was on Sunday mornings. I spent at least seventy-five percent of my income on buying pot, not including gas money. I had it bad! I even rode with him on my days off, so that I could continue getting high. I'd hang out in my uncle's apartment on Southside Richmond, at Hampshire Apartments located on Belt Blvd. During these off days, I would eat at McDonald's, smoke pot, cigarettes, and watch TV.

In 1976, there was a warning about potentially lethal marijuana being on the black market that had been tainted with a chemical called "paraquat". My uncle, who was also a drug dealer, insisted that we buy our pot from him, for safety reasons. I was too foolish to realize that he would not have known whether or not his marijuana was tainted. But we considered him an authority on street drugs. If we found ourselves low on money and pot, we would steal it from him. My uncle glamorized the drug culture, and was enamored of the fast-paced wheeling and dealing lifestyle of this illicit way of life. The thought of buying and selling large quantities of pot made his eyes beam with excitement and also made our eyes beam at the prospect of having a seemingly unending supply of marijuana. Pot became like gold to me— it was treasure. Little did I know that I was replacing God by becoming enamored of drugs. I went from praising God to praising drugs. We would rate pot for its quality, texture and place of origin. During this particular summer, I went from having joy at the visionary prospect of becoming a successful man that God would use mightily, to having excitement at the visionary prospect of buying marijuana plantations in Peru. My visions of the future changed, because my spiritual connection had changed. I mentioned earlier in this book that the biblical word for sorcery comes from the Greek word "pharmakeia", meaning drugs. Drug abuse is a form of the practice of witchcraft, which is provoked and influenced by spirits of darkness, whose dictator is Satan. Though I didn't know it, I was practicing sorcery, and perpetuated it in the communities were I lived and visited, by the using and purchasing various mood-and mind-altering substances. Spirits can influence the way we think and perceive things and ourselves. Thus, illicit drugs can open us up to the influence of demonic beings. This is why we see many crimes, from thievery to murder, saturate the drug culture and those areas of our communities where this culture flourishes. It is written, "The thief cometh not, but for to steal, and to kill, and to destroy" (John 10: 10).

As far as drugs affecting my heart and mind spiritually, it is evident that my focus at this time was drug possession and use. It was a treasure to me. Jesus said that where a man's treasure is, there will his heart be also (Matthew 6:21). My treasure has changed; therefore, the place where my treasure resided had changed. Jesus requested that we should build up for ourselves treasures in heaven where they would not, nor could not, decay (Matthew 6:20). But, he warned that we were not to store up for ourselves corruptible things. Yet, I went from focusing on incorruptible things to minding things that were perishable, and made *me* susceptible to perishing, that is, made every aspect of my life corruptible and dysfunctional. I wondered whether I had lost my salvation.

I thank God for school beginning in September. With the new school term beginning, this summer's smoke fest ended, and I was able to concentrate on academic things and upcoming sports activities. As my pot smoking decreased, my refocusing on Christ increased. I was able to refocus on visions of a potential life in Christ Jesus. But I did not make the connection between the various problem areas in my life, especially with the increasingly dysfunctional relationship with my parents, and the embracing of drugs. At this stage in my association with drugs, I had on occasions tested other substances, such as powdered cocaine, hashish, which is an intensified marijuana residue, LSD, and various forms of speed. While my drug use had lessened, on occasion, I would drive up to my cousin's dorm in the hope that he would have some pot. We sometimes, when without drugs, would visit a friend, who lived in my general neighborhood, and would experiment with sniffing various aerosol fumes. This was accomplished in a most dangerous way, because it involved using fire. I again thank God for his mercy, because we might have destroyed his home, and caused permanent brain damage to ourselves. THANK YOU LORD!

Although I managed to maintain a very good grade point average, graduated on time, and was accepted at various prestigious colleges, I secretly lived a double and unstable life. This revelation proves that God's Word is true in every way. It is written in the epistle of James, the brother of Jesus, that "a *double minded man is unstable in all his ways*" (James 1:8) KJV.

I was not only unstable, but tossed back and forth from Church and school activity to small periods of drug activity.

I was so arrogant and promoting about the pleasures of being high, especially on marijuana, that I did a gross disservice to a good friend. One Friday night, during a post football game dance at our Community Center, I introduced my friend to smoking marijuana. We, and several of our peers, went behind the building in a dimly lit area, to smoke some joints. My friend followed us, but was hesitant to participate. I, sad to say, was very tenacious in insisting that he try it. Finally, he gave in. We smoked so much in a short time that we began to laugh uncontrollably. (Note: As of this writing, some twenty-five years later, all of us who were smoking reefer on that night behind our community center, are living mightily for Christ, except for the one whom I persuaded to try drugs. Since I've been a fervent minister of Christ, I have on several occasions witnessed to my old friend of the power of God to pull down strongholds. However, he remains in bondage). It is ironic how it took only a few minutes of tenacious persuasion to convince him to try marijuana. Yet, after several occasions and many hours of fervent testimony and ministering the Word of God, in love, as well as my beseeching him for forgiveness, he has not broken loose from his addictions. His pot smoking, as did mine, eventually lead to alcohol abuse, and harder drug addictions.

I continue to pray for my friend's release from this bondage, believing that God will lead him to deliverance. I am also thankful for God's mercy and forgiveness for what I did twenty-five years ago. For, unless Christ is merciful to me, I would surely perish for this sin. Jesus stated in the Gospels that whosoever will offend a young person that it would be better that a Millstone be hung around their necks and they be drowned into the depths of the sea (Matthew 18:6). This statement is symbolic of the inescapable judgment of Christ for any unrepentant soul that has caused a young person, who believes in him, to stumble.

The struggle between my flesh and the Spirit was periodically fought as I walked into adulthood. My graduating from high school marked the beginning of total freedom from youthful authorities. I became free to be the final authority in all the decisions that I would make in my life.

## Chapter 14

# The College Years

*Falling and failing will be the result of a dangerous*
*mix of independence and irresponsibilty*

After graduation from high school, I had decided to attend The College of William and Mary, in Williamsburg, Virginia. I was nervous and unsure of several things in my life, such as my relationship with Cathy, my preparedness for a college of this academic reputation, and the viability of my relationship with God. I wanted to walk with Christ during these forthcoming years; for I sensed not an easy time in acquiring good success, as did my cousin at VUU.

I prayed much those weeks before I left for college, which was only an approximate thirty-minute drive from my home in Charles City County. In all honesty, I knew that I wasn't ready, specifically due to my addiction to marijuana, and my lack of maturity to deal with the separation from Cathy. During that summer after our high school graduation, we had become more involved. A greater bond, however dysfunctional, was fostered between us, due to our increased sexual activity and decrease in other fruitful friendships during that summer. For me, much of that time was spent smoking pot, and chasing behind Cathy. It was all about fulfilling the lust of the flesh. Strangely enough, she didn't know that I had become a chronic marijuana user. She never knew that I was high when I came to see her, though I never smoked when I was with her. I began carrying Visine eye drops, and tried not to drink alcohol, which I knew would be a dead give-away. Cathy had once smelled alcohol on my breath and went ballistic! She warned that the quickest way to destroy our relationship was for me to become a user of alcoholic beverages. I think that she never, at that time, considered that drug abuse was even a possibility for me. Nevertheless, the bond that I felt to our relationship was very strong, and I didn't deal well with the prospect of leaving her for long periods of time. Cathy, being more mature emotionally, fared better in the change that took place in our lives after that summer. She took on several jobs, to support our son Jeffrey; began taking courses at J. Sergeant Reynolds Community College and Virginia Commonwealth University. Also, she was accepted to Richmond Memorial School of Nursing, and eventually became a Registered Nurse. I was truly impressed, and secretly intimidated, by her tenacity to survive and succeed.

On the day that I arrived on the campus of W&M, I quickly found the dorm in which I was to abide— Dupont dorm for incoming freshmen. My Parents were beaming with pride and joy, for I never told them of my insecurities. Upon my mother making my bed, and saying a prayer, her and dad soon left. I laid on my bed, meditating about the Lord, my future, Cathy, our son Jeff, and whether I could go without smoking pot for a semester. I had started smoking cigarettes habitually, unbeknown to Cathy or my parents, and thought this would be a viable substitute for pot.

Within the hour, I decided to try to find some of my high school peers who also made W&M their choice. I had entered into the W&M undergraduate program, along with Faye, whom I took to our junior prom, because Cathy was pregnant with Jeff; and Angela, our Senior Class Valedictorian— also my relative and nearby neighbor at home in Ruthville; and Kent, who was always friendly. After a brief visit, I went back to my dorm. As I strolled through the building I met a student named Darryl. We instantly became fast friends. Within a few minutes he discovered that we both were marijuana users. I believe we actually secured an appointment to get high together later that day.

Afterwards, I went back to my room to see if I would run into my roommate whom I had not met. Sure enough he was mulling around. We introduced ourselves, and he immediately left. I sensed that he was not comfortable with me, a black student, as his roommate. On the following semester he changed room assignments, of which I was glad. I found him to be untidy, and filthy in the way he kept our room, though we rarely saw each other. He rarely slept in our room, living most of his time with his friends.

While unpacking my clothes on that first day of college, I began to smell a faint odor of marijuana coming from across the hallway. I came outside to investigate, and walking in front of my door was a student from Hawaii. He was not smoking pot, but was obviously high, and carrying a Tall Boy, which is an extra large can of beer. He stopped and introduced himself, and indicated that he was about to visit my neighbor across the hall from me. He asked if I got high, and I said yes. He invited me in to the room, asked the residents if I could get high with them, and they agreed. Due to these students being quite better off than I, our friendship fostered four years of a seemingly endless supply of drugs, especially marijuana. I became very close friends with one of the students in that room that day, named Perry. He was also a chronic pot user. He was very welcoming and generous with his marijuana, and sometimes supplied me with pot, free of charge. We smoked each day during that semester, without fail. I smoked with him daily, and also with Daryl, upperclassmen, football, and basketball players with whom I became friends. Besides classes, and the cafeteria, every other place that I chose to visit was inundated with drugs. At the time I felt accepted and in the mix, but in reality I was being set up for academic failure. During that first semester, I lacked the maturity to make wise decisions as to my behavior and the will power to resist the temptation of drug abuse. This was due to denying myself the study of the Word. I did bring my Bible to college, and put it in a visible place. I felt a strong unction to read the Gospels, but was subsequently and simultaneously bombarded with offers to smoke pot and guzzle beer. I didn't realize it then, but I was being presented with a choice to seek wisdom or foolishness, or, more specifically, given the opportunity for life or death spiritually. In the book of Deuteronomy of the Old Testament God inspired his prophet Moses to set before the people a choice. He stated " ... *that I have set before you life and death, blessing and cursing: therefore choose life*"—Deuteronomy 30: 19 (KJV).

*God* was compelling me to choose life and blessings. However, I made choices that eventually led to my being cursed in many areas of my life, including college, my lack of a relationship with Jeff, losing my relationship with Cathy, and being the cause of much heartache to my parents.

Also, I made consistently bad choices in the kind of course load I took. I foolishly decided what I would major in before I realized my aptitudes. I had decided to go premed. I went to my college-selected advisor, who happened to be an Italian foreign language professor. For the life of me I could never understand a word he said, but I was either too high or intimidated to confess it. Thus, without advice, I decided my own course load, and it was a killer. I chose to take, in my first semester, and without a sufficient background, Calculus 101, Biology 101, Physics 101, and Chemistry 101. I was so out of touch with my academic abilities, that I actually thought I could successfully pass these courses, and with little study. I was living in a fantasyland sure enough. I was so out of my league in knowledge of these courses that when I walked into biology class on that first day, the professor said, "since we were all W&M students, and known to be among the best and the brightest, let us all start on chapter ten of the text". I thought that I would have an anxiety attack. I went back to my room and looked at chapter one. I realized that of all the science and biology that I studied in high school, it didn't even begin to approach what was in the first chapter of that book. There was hardly a word that I recognized from my high school studies. This was the same experience with each subject. Consequently, along with my excessive drug use, I failed each of those courses. I also took a Government 101 course that semester which I should have passed, but didn't, due to lack of study and, again, chronic marijuana use. The only thing I passed that semester was a Physical Education course. I never showed anyone those grades, and I received a warning that if my grade point average did not improve by the end of the spring semester, that I would be put on probation and asked to sit out for the forthcoming fall semester. I was quite distraught and ashamed at my lack of effort and unwise choices.

When I packed up to go home for Christmas vacation, I went into daily prayer, saturated myself with the Word of God, and repented from the use of drugs and alcohol. I went back to college in mid January 1979, with a new and faithful outlook. I knew I would have temptations to use pot, but with prayer and a commitment to keep my vow to God, I was confident to not use drugs again. On that spring semester, I studied hard, went to each class, avoided drugging places and friends, and went home on many weekends to attend worship services. That semester ended with me passing all my courses, most with B's. I sensed that God wanted me to test His Word to see that it was true. Consequently, I experienced that God is faithful to His Word. It is written in the Psalms of the Old Testament that "Blessed *is the man that walketh not in the counsel of the ungodly, nor standeth in the way of sinners, nor sitteth in the seat of the scornful. But his delight is in the law of the LORD; and in his law doth he meditate day and night. And he shall be like a tree planted by the rivers of water, that bringeth forth his fruit in his season; and his leaf also shall not wither; and <u>whatsoever he doeth shall prosper</u>" (Psalm 1: 1-3) KJV.*

## Chapter 15

# Same Folks, Same Strokes

*"But it is happened unto them according to the true proverb, the dog is turned to his own vomit again, and the sow that was washed to her wallowing in in the mire."*
*(2nd Peter 2:22 KJV)*

I was very elated about the academic success I had on the second semester, such that I celebrated with a blow away marijuana smoke fest. Upon the completion of my last exam, I, with Perry, Darryl, and some other chronic users, tried to make up for lost time. I didn't realize my re-emergence into a state of addiction. I had reverted back to the time before I made that vow to God. But how was this possible? Well, I made a vow not to do drugs or drink; and to avoid tempting people and places, for a specified time, i.e. that freshman spring semester. However, I did not make a decision to repent permanently from those destructive ways, nor did I know that there was a difference.

I was experiencing much happiness due to my academic success, and uplifted in my confidence level. God had been truly faithful to me, and I saw first hand how the law of His inspired Word is true and unfailing. Yet, in the celebratory way that I responded to this happy time, I perverted the joy of the Lord that I gleaned from my short-lived obedience. Because of this perverted response to Christ's favor, I repeated that same pattern of foolishness, even worse. Though I do not believe that every statement of Narcotics Anonymous (N.A.) and Alcoholics Anonymous (A.A.) is expedient, yet, I am in agreement with one of their several precepts. They teach that when a person leaves the throws of addiction, but returns, even after years of being clean, he begins at the same level of abuse as before, or worse. (I am convinced that a Christian based drug and alcohol ministry\ program will better benefit the body and the spirit, in that, it will be profitable for the release of a drugging lifestyle, and for the salvation of one's soul, through Jesus Christ, our Lord. After all, it was Jesus that said, "For what shall it profit a man, if he shall gain the whole world, and lose his own soul?"[Mark *8:36 KJV*])

I went into that summer of 1979, with all that fruitful joy, turned into foolish arrogance. I procured a job working for Richmond Memorial hospital, in Richmond, VA. I was employed as a medication runner, distributing the hospital's pharmacy's meds to the various nurse's stations. I spent that whole summer in a persistent mental fog. I smoked so much, that I don't remember coming down from the "high" that entire summer. I negated the prayer life that developed over that spring semester, and also the study of God's Word, for which I had acquired so great an affection.

Cathy and I had broken off our relationship. Yet, in my arrogance, I was confident that we would, over that summer, restore it. (Six months earlier, Cathy admitted to a new relationship that she had formed with a Henrico County police officer. I was devastated. I didn't know how to deal with the rejection, and up to that point in my life, had never known broken heartedness. Emotionally, I was a complete wreck. I showered myself in the drug culture, not referring to anything that I had learned from the study of the scriptures in earlier youth. I even considered suicide). Note: The option of suicide is a prevalent decision among some teenagers with dysfunctional relationships, whether they are parental or romantic. I suggest that teenagers seek competent Christian counseling, submerge themselves in prayer and the study of the word; and seek helpful complimentary Christian-related books. I suggest that you seek out the various books authored by the well-known Dr. James Dobson of "Focus on the Family". His books have helped my wife and me tremendously. Two of his books, <u>Dare to discipline</u> and<u> Love must be tough</u> will be immensely helpful in finding answers to one's problems that his books address. Obtain Dr. Dobson's books that address your particular concerns.

As mentioned, I became confident that Cathy and I would return to our relationship. I didn't know how this was to play out, but I guessed that Cathy would be impressed with my confident attitude about my future, i.e. becoming a doctor. Also, I knew that Cathy was very conscious, though not always tenacious in her obedience, of God's will for how we ought to live as believers. So, I believed that her relationship with this man, who was much older, and was known to not practice fidelity, would be short lived. I believed that the Lord would lead her to the conviction that she was in an unacceptable affair.

I did not know where Cathy lived in the beginning of that summer. I knew that she was still in nursing school, but I didn't know what direction her life had taken. Then, one day I reported for work on the 7am shift. I got to work early to eat breakfast in the hospital's basement cafeteria. As I was in line, I felt someone tap me on my back. It was Cathy! She was all decked out in her new student nurse's uniform. She looked stunning. I was so happy to see her that I could hardly contain myself. But I also sensed sadness in my spirit. She looked vibrant and happy. I knew there was something special in her life, and it wasn't me. We subsequently ate breakfast together, but she asked that it not seem as though we knew one another. I asked why that was necessary. She said that other staff knew that she was now dating one of the security staff at the hospital and didn't want to jeopardize in by anyone revealing that she knew me. Again, I was cut to the quick! My heart was broken. This time it was more due to my arrogant suppositions than with my lack of preparation for this new revelation. She told me, without hesitation, that there was nothing more important in her life than this new boyfriend. She was hopelessly in love, with no prospect of recanting. A few days later I saw both of them leaving the hospital building, hand in hand. I wanted to quit my job at that point and run away from life. I remember that my stomach ached that whole summer; and I experienced no relief from the pain. But, I decided to keep the job. I wanted to show Cathy that I had matured and grown beyond our past, though it was the furthest thing from the truth. I thought, in the back of my mind, that if Cathy knew how promising of a career I was destined to have, then her desire for a secure and prosperous life would bend her back into my direction. And in some ways this happened later in the summer. She showed me some interest at a distance, but did not relinquish her then present relationship. I felt she wanted to keep me in range just to see how my plans progressed. Nevertheless, I drowned my sorrows in drugs and partying with friends. I dovetailed deep into music ballads, believing they would help me deal with my woes. I would ride in my faded blue ford, smoking and listening to soul music AM radio stations, and periodically visiting friends who were avid music buffs and chronic pot smokers. This listening to love ballads was actually a bad thing emotionally, because it caused me to not be released from my internal torment. It is written in Proverbs 25:20, *"...like vinegar poured on soda, is one who sings songs to a heavy heart." (NIV)*

I tried to get over Cathy as best I could, but I was secretly depressed and unmotivated. For the next three years of my college career, I barely held on to my student standing, destined to fail, wasting all those years accomplishing nothing; and living in a drug induced fantasy world. Upon reflection, I can see that drugs kept me from regaining focus on Christ. Satan's tool of substance abuse has been successful against those who might otherwise submerge themselves in Christ, because of the ability of drugs to make a person powerless to the expedient thing for their life.

Due to a non-drug related circumstance, I finally saw how powerful drug use affected my life at this time. During this summer of working in the pharmacy at RMH, I was falsely accused of making verbal advances to one of the female pharmacist. I believe that she stereotyped me to be one of those men that tried to make advances to every woman. She judged me falsely. I had some bad behavior, but trying to develop a new love affair out of loneliness, or male hormonal motivation was not my desire, nor did I ever attempt such things. Being a young black man, who worked during light staffing, made her feel uncomfortable. Her fear was due to stereotyping or racial prejudice. Subsequently, the department supervisor called me into his office to address this issue. He refused to tell me who made this accusation. I became offended by his insistence that these statements were true, and wanted to know how he could justify his position on this matter without me being able to address and know my accuser. He insisted that I sign a letter stating that I would not have any non-work related conversation with any female staff. This was surmountable to me admitting guilt. That supervisor said that if I did not sign the letter then he would dismiss me from my job. I knew that this was a case of discrimination and duress, in that he threatened my job. I became inwardly furious. However, I was inundated with thoughts of not being able to see Cathy each day, or able to purchase the large amounts of marijuana that I used daily. Mostly, it was the pot issue that caused me to give in to the supervisor's request. I realized then how dangerous a problem I had with drugs. I was willing to be persecuted falsely for the sake of maintaining my level of addiction. This reality was now apparent, but was not enough to motivate me to quit. I am deeply ashamed of the kind of loyalty I gave to a drugging lifestyle. This kind of loyalty should be reserved for God. It is this kind of perverted loyalty to idol gods, (and drug addiction is idol worship), that provokes God to jealousy. It is written in the 20th chapter of Exodus verses 3 and 5 "(3) *Thou shalt have no other gods before me. (5) Thou shalt not bow down thyself to them, nor serve them: <u>for I the Lord thy God am a jealous God</u>...*"

I now was in the depths of despair. I went from a semester of promises fulfilled, to curses abounding. My joy had turned into sorrow.

# Chapter 16

# Storm Tossed

*"A double minded man is unstable in all his ways"*
*(James 1:8 KJV)*

This same pattern of behavior persisted for the next three years. While pursuing a life of drugging and slothful living, I went through periods of fervently seeking Christ and asking Him to make intercession on behalf of my unfaithful walk. I'd beseech Him to put me on a right path. In my heart I knew that I had to stop the drugging and visiting people who knew not Christ. But my heart had other lusts that preempted the lust for Christ, namely, drugs and Cathy. I was living a double-minded existence. During the next three years while at the College of William and Mary, I had temporary, but unannounced visits to Cathy's place in Richmond. Also, she visited me at my apartment in Williamsburg. It seems we were curious about how progressive our lives were in between the months of not communicating to one another. It was as competition over whose life was turning out the best. At that point in our lives she was winning "big time". Her relationship with her boyfriend was moving forward, although Cathy and I would once or twice a year have secret romantic liaisons. I perceived, that for Cathy, the secret rendezvous was adventurous. It possibly gave her a sense of power that was absent in her present relationship. For me, it was a small attempt at regaining a lost relationship. I pretended to like the secrecy, but I really abhorred it. I knew that this did not honor her present relationship, and unfaithful behavior exemplified a part of Cathy that concerned me. We would many times deceive ourselves by rationalizing a need to be updated on Jeffrey's life. Almost always our meetings were filled with arguments and contentions. I often thought that Cathy merely wanted to vent her frustration at the turns her life had taken. I was not sure whether or not she had forgiven me for getting her pregnant. Also, I felt that she wanted to find out if I had another love interest. She was not comfortable with me having another relationship, though she was involved with another man. Cathy told me that she felt I would one day fall in love after she had done all the work in teaching me how to treat a women. She was concerned about being slighted in such a way.

My life was very unstable at this point. By the end of my fourth year in college I had utterly failed to accomplish any of the so-called goals that I set. I made no real plans to accomplish anything. Therefore, failure ensued. In May of 1982, the College of William and Mary sent me a certified letter stating that I had not fulfilled the requirements for continuing my education at that institution. The College only gives a student, on the degree program, ten semesters to graduate; and my ten semesters were now spent. I was showered in disappointment, but I confessed that I had brought it on myself. It was now time for me to step out on my own, and get a real job. Oh, how foolish a thought! I had received a letter of recommendation from W&M to submit to any college that I would apply. A prudent man would have taken advantage of the opportunity to continue his education elsewhere. But, I told myself that I would have continued in the same drug induced mindset at some other college. So, I opted to go to work. I know I felt very much the failure, but said in my foolish pride that I would not let my family and friends see that I was "squirming" my way to another college or university. Is that foolish or what?

Strangely enough, no one suggested that I continue with the pursuit of higher learning. I guess no one knew how to approach me concerning this matter, including my parents.

I had decided to pursue a job rather than my most recent professed goal— a degree in political science.

It is interesting how I went from pre-med to political science; from fervently pursuing drugs, to periodically seeking God, and tenaciously following after Cathy, yet spending months on end avoiding her. I was truly the epitome of an unstable and double-minded man.

My first job after leaving college was at the Long John Silver seafood restaurant. I made myself believe that I could progress to a prosperous future with this job opportunity. But all that I had done was finance my drug habit, while grossly avoiding responsible behavior.

In some ways I wanted to embrace my family, but shamefacedness was the order of the day. Therefore, I submerged myself in either loneliness or keeping company with my drugging friends. I also wanted to become involved in the church again, but the issue of shame and failure were ever present before me. After all, my church family was so proud of me, and I believed I let them down. They had doted over me with well wishes and congratulatory praises. I guessed that they wouldn't know what to say to me. I didn't want to put them in that position. But, sadly, the real reason was that I was unwilling to give up my drug habit. My lack of prudence was directly related to drugging. If my mental state had not been under the influence of narcotics, I believe a decision to transfer to another college would have been made; and I would have fared better in my inclination to go back to church.

## Chapter 17

# Stolen High

*"Let him that stole steal no more... (Ephesians 4:28 KJV)*

As I began a career of gaining and losing jobs, I acquired the uncomplimentary habit of pilfering money and/or goods from my employers. Along with this drug habit, I had become a thief. The remaining good brain cells that I retained were used to devise ways by which I could steal from employers. Mostly, I opted to take money from the till of my register. I did not steal the money in such a way as to create a shortage, but usually defrauded my employer by falsifying returns or deleting sales from the day's receipts. Many positions that I held were either managerial, or supervisory. My pretense of living a Christian life, professing Christ to my co-workers and bosses, allowed me to be viewed as an honest man, though I was not. I can say that the habit of defrauding was thoroughly sown into me from my college days. My parents were called on many times to help me buy school supplies, but I used the funds to purchase marijuana on almost every occasion. This form of craftiness was carried into my post college working years. I can't begin to remember the total amount stolen from jobs that gave me their trust.

At first, the decision to steal money was not a consideration. The fear of being caught was too strong. However, My income could not keep up with my chronic pot use. I do not say "life style", because I lacked a style of life. I simply smoked pot, went to work, drank beer while smoking after work, and slept. I repeated the same cycle each day. I remember the first time I stole from my employer. "Jones'in" hard for a bag of pot, having little more than a few cents, I waited after the store manager departed, then saw my chance to defraud. I voided several sales of new customers that came into the seafood restaurant where I worked. Knowing that the customers wouldn't require a receipt, I took the chance to void their tickets. I pilfered about $17.00, having enough for a "dime bag"($10) of refer, $3.00 for gas, $1.00 for a quart of beer, $1.00 for cigarettes, and $2.00 for food, so as to satisfy the munchies that I routinely experienced. This sort of thing continued throughout fourteen months of employment. Eventually, I was terminated. I believe that my immediate supervisor knew I had become dishonest and searched for reasons to fire me. My thieving antics continued on jobs where I was given managerial opportunities, which ultimately resulted in my quitting or being terminated. I would no longer try to budget my money to accommodate my habit. It became easy to reconcile in myself that I could simply take it from the cash register at work. If I happened to find a moment of reflection on the fact that my stealing was sin against God and men, or experience a window of sobriety, then, I would experience a time of conviction. I told myself that I would replace the money on the very next payday. But, this never transpired. If I had recompensed the money, which would have been the righteous thing to do, this would not have lessened my sin, nor, without repentance and God's forgiveness, would recompense have the spiritually cleansing effect that I sought. Should I have bothered to make recompense? Oh yes! Although I was not yet repentant, I would have put in process the righting of my wrongs. I would have shown an outward display of an inward desire to walk in a kind of consciousness of God. This would have been a step toward being mindful that my thieving ways were abhorrent, thereby eventually being loosed from my weakness for stealing. Also, even more abhorrent, was my continued professing that I walked with Christ, allowing me to be exposed as a liar. If I had only acknowledged Paul's writing in 2nd Corinthians 4:2, which says, "But have renounced the hidden things of dishonesty, not walking in craftiness, nor handling the word of God deceitfully; but by manifestation of the truth commending ourselves to every man's conscience in the sight of God." (KJV)

It may not be the usual way that one comes to Christ with a sincere heart, but for some, doing the right thing can lead to the depth of conviction we need for true, heart-felt repentance. It seems that the practice of walking in righteousness is a kind of seed sowing within our spirit, such that the effort of walking right before the Lord leads us into a new nature that develops as we allow ourselves to be changed by God. He compels us to let Him make us new creations. God will provoke us to think thoughts of righteousness, such that we will began to be loosed from a fleshly perspective and give way to a Godly perspective, i.e. righteous thinking. It is written, we are not to be *"… conformed to this world: but be transformed by the renewing of your mind…"* (Romans 12:2) KJV.

## Chapter 18

# The Fog Years

*"They have wandered like blind men in the streets;*
*they have polluted themselves with blood..."*
*(Lamentations 4:14 KJV)*

The Fog Years", May 1982 thru October 1988, was when I stagnated in a perpetual, drug induced, mental fog. My sensory perception was less acute than normal. I was not quite connected to the realities of the world around me. Often, when I talked to people, my hearing and understanding seemed muffled; and all encounters were in dream-state. There were a few days, and I mean a very few, that I wasn't high. But they were so rare that it would be weeks, months, and even years between sober days. Oh, what a sad and wasteful time. And yet, even the rare abstinent days were fogged, because my body was so polluted with marijuana that I remained in a fog-like mental state. It had gotten so bad that after I left an environment, or finished a conversation, I wasn't sure in my own consciousness whether I had been there or done that. I felt medium certain, but not completely sure of what I experienced. I suspect that this was not like an alcoholic "black out", but rather a question of whether my experience, or parts of my experience, were imagination. Also, I pondered which parts of my experiences were real and which were imagined.

The question of whether illusions blended with my experiences was often considered. I remember one particular day, while standing in my parent's den, having a conversation with my mother about drugs, God, Jeff, Cathy, or life in general, of which I'm unsure. The peculiar thing about this time is that after I was on my way to wherever, I couldn't decide if my mother was standing or sitting while she spoke, or standing on a chair cleaning the clock or drapes. I couldn't decide whether my dad was in the room. I was not even sure whether any conversation with my mother had transpired. I do remember feeling that there was a thin film on my eyes that made things seem as if I received my experiences through a veil. This happened in almost every circumstance of my life.

My interrelating with others, especially those who cared much for me, often seemed surreal. As mentioned, this was the same experience with Cathy, with whom I talked more often than anyone. Though my reasoning told me that I did have experiences with Cathy, however, my experience was like a dreamlike distortion of reality. I would visit Cathy in Richmond, Va. during the latter part of the week and weekends. I'd get high on pot, usually drink one beer, and sometimes take some acid on the trek to her apartment. Often times, she would be at one of several jobs. I would proceed to locate her to let her know that I was in town. Usually, she granted me access to the apartment. I mostly continued getting high until a few hours before she came home. Interestingly, Cathy seemed unaware of this.

Upon Cathy's arrival, we would either go out to eat, dine in, have small talk, or argue. If I made it through the verbal fighting without being thrown out, then, we would proceed with foreplay, and ultimately give in to the throws of passion. Each time, Cathy and I would go through a torment like guilt over the sexual sins of the night, thus allowing me an excuse to leave under the guise of not giving place to further temptation. But the true motive of my heart was to escape so as to use more drugs. Also believing that I secured redemption with Cathy, while at the same time satisfying my veracious appetite for marijuana. I was not mindful to seek the redemptive work of our Lord Jesus Christ.

Just as I sit in my old faded blue Ford Montego, rolling several joints, and preparing to buy a Coors Lite from a nearby 7-11, my memory would become uncertain. I knew, with marijuana, that there was short-term memory loss. However, this was not my forgetting what had just happened, but it was my losing grip as to whether that which I *was* remembering actually happened. As I cruised eastward on interstate 64, heading toward home in Charles City County, I quickly smoked the first joint, while swallowing great gulps of beer. It quenched the burning sensation I often felt in my throat from the hot smoke. (I would hold the smoke in my lungs for long periods, so to get the maximum effect). By the time I neared the Bottoms Bridge exit in New Kent County, I'd become even less sure of having visited Cathy. Consequently, at that point, I'd turn around and go back to the west end of Henrico County, starting the night over. I would return to Cathy's apartment, knock on the door, and awaken her out of sleep. I would never provoke much conversation, but simply ask to stay the night while keeping a quiet demeanor, afraid that any exposure of confusion would make Cathy question my sanity, thus, destroying an already shaky relationship.

Reflecting on those years, I was never unsure about my get high experiences. I always remembered when, where, and with whom I got high. Sad to say, staying high had become a normal state of being for me.

Let me expose the other truth of the matter. The fog in which I lived during those post college years was a kind of blindness that occurred daily. As with a blind person not being completely sure of things about them so was I unsure of the reality of experiences that encapsulated my life. Also, this blinding fog symbolized the lack of clarity that I showed in not recognizing the societal effects of my drug participation.

The nation watched the criminal element increase dramatically during the 1980's, and particularly in the city of Richmond. Nationally, Richmond ranked extremely high for murders per capita during several periods of the 80's and 90's. At that time I couldn't see that my marijuana purchases aided in the promotion of a wicked drug culture, especially in the African American communities. With this evil sub-culture came a plethora of crimes and criminals, ever increasing. I helped make the drug game profitable; therefore, I had a part in the criminal elements and violent crimes that invaded the entire city. Although I didn't kill or rob anyone of my own direct experience, the money I spent helped to strengthen and advance Satan's agenda in that society. Therefore the blood of those young black boys and black men was also on my hands. God knows if some had not been murdered, they may have become priests and prophets. The prophet Jeremiah writes of a truth in the book of Lamentations 4:14, "They have wandered as blind men in the streets, they have polluted themselves with blood…" (KJV)

In the summer of 1988 there were some mob-style murders in the city. It involved approximately six people being murdered while tied up and blindfolded. It was on the news for several days and in the newspapers. Although I read about this, I didn't know the relationship it had to me. One of the young men that was murdered was the marijuana dealer from whom my friend Ben and I purchased our pot. We bought lots of it, thus helping him come to the conclusion that drug dealing was profitable and a worthy occupation. We edified his belief that the drug game was the way to prosperity, notwithstanding the evil that resulted in its activities. Drug dealers develop an idolizing love for power, the prestige of their culture, and money. But evil works is a direct consequence of these ambitions. The Bible says that their "love of money is the root of all evil... and pierced themselves through with many sorrows."(1st Timothy 6:10 KJV)

Not only did they pierce themselves spiritually, but also their deeds fostered piercing of their flesh by way of murderous gunplay. I speak not only of them, but also of myself. I too gained a love of money, so as to gain access to more drugs. I did whatever I could for that almighty dollar. It was called the almighty dollar because it was idolized as a god. Furthermore, I felt pierced in my heart when hearing that the man, as well as the others, were those from whom I bought marijuana. So, I felt partly responsible for the lifestyle that ultimately fostered his death. I had played a part in creating the atmosphere for violent crime, not only in the city of Richmond, but wherever my dollars went in the earth to the pursuit of building up the drug trade.

I felt that my connection to the murders of these people was even closer after my friend Ben explained that we had frequented the area where these people lived and had businesses. These were people that I met through him. I talked with some of them and became part of their scenery during the recent summers. However, after hearing of their tragedy, I was happy that my connection to those folks did not flourish. Nevertheless, my involvement in the drug trade was instrumental in bringing about a greedy and idolizing subculture which begat young black men that killed and died for their god— "Mammon".

During the late '80's, there was a period of decrease in the availability of pot. This set me up for the trial of a new, smokable drug called free-base cocaine. The events that resulted from this tool of the prince of the devils only increased the volatile activities of the drug culture to new heights, such that murders became commonplace. I sensed that the killings of young black men and women were becoming less horrific to the public, and even made for a desensitizing of their emotions to senseless murders.

## Chapter 19

# Cracking Up the Family

*"For the lips of a strange woman drop as an honeycomb, and her mouth is smother than oil... Remove thy way far from her, and come not nigh the door of her house... Lest strangers be filled with thy wealth; and thy labours be in the house of a stranger." Proverbs 5: 3,8,10 (KJV)*

My friends, Pete, Charlton and I would sit in their apartment and watch music videos on cable TV, either the BET or VH-1 channel. There was one, entitled <u>Crack killed Applejack</u>, which caught my attention. I thought how sad it was to experience a tragedy of a loved one, and feel powerless to stop the progression of a conspiracy that had its birth in the spiritual realm. Even then I felt the foreboding of a death grip in the black community. However, in arrogance, I thought I had escaped the heightening dangers of the newest in the drug culture—"crack".

Some of my friends and I had gone as far as lacing pot with powdered cocaine, thinking that it would add a heightened boost to our high. We never believed for a moment that this would lead to free-base or crack cocaine use. Many claimed that it was harmless and different, with a kind of euphoria that was unparalleled by any high experienced. But some claimed it was very taxing on their body, mind, job, family, and especially their marriage. I began seeing their marriages fall apart with all speed. Separation was the order of the day. There were highly unusual behaviors exemplified by these men. During 1985, on cold winter days, I watched our friends gather at the apartment of my homeboys from Charles City, Charlton and Pete. They came in sweaty, hyper, jittery, and looking gaunt. I don't believe Charlton had ever dabbled in crack or free-base, but others of us didn't have his mindset of resolve. At the time I didn't know why they were acting strange, many of them being musicians in local clubs or traveling bands. I noticed that over a very few months they began to talk about being separated from their wives, breaking up with girl friends, or alienated from their parents. They all seem to have the same domestic outcomes. Also their drinking increased as their pot smoking drastically decreased. Later, I observed that this was a sign of a transfer from one drug, marijuana, to another, free-base cocaine. As a person becomes addicted to crack or free-base, and if they use marijuana, the cost of both is usually not accomadatable, nor is the desire for pot as prevalent as before. The addict's mind is absorbed with obtaining the pleasure of that extreme high at any cost. These men, I noticed, seemed to no longer have any loyalty to their female counterparts. They didn't want relationships with any other lover but crack.

We called cocaine "Girl". The logic was that it gave you all the pleasures of a magnificent lover, with no other motive but to satisfy your greatest euphorically orgasmic high. Only a sexual experience of erotic proportions could compare. This was another problem of crack addiction; it made one hungry for more euphoria in their party escapes. Thus, crack users often integrate illicit and perverted sex into their crack using lifestyle. These men would satisfy their sexual fantasies by using women with crack habits, and performing all kinds of gross pornographic acts. One night, as we sit in my friend's apartment smoking pot, several of these men came in, partially drunk, bragging on what they had done to a woman the day before. On this particular occasion, I noticed that Pete and Charlton seemed perturbed and uncomfortable. I was not knowledgeable of what these men had done, but my friends were. Those men had gone to the point, and I believe while using crack, of having anal sex with her. They ran a "train" on her as it were. Trains, in street terms, are men, in almost a sexually assaulting style, having back-to-back continuous sex with a woman. Furthermore, in this case, they sodomized her, and bragged that the woman screamed to the top of her voice, and sobbed with all sadness. They confessed that they witnessed her anguishing pain, but continued for hours pouring into her more drugs and alcohol. They eventually took her to the hospital where she received care. They joked that they caused her swelling hemorrhoids and bleeding. Why did she allow this? Well, the crack is like a god to the user, and most worshippers love their gods more than their own self. Their gods are the drugs and the lusts of their own addictive flesh.

The second part of the transference of pot addiction to crack addiction is an increase in alcohol use. It is used as a quick and cheap high. The crack addict will run out of drugs, and go through times when coke or money is scarce. Thus, cheap beer, wine and liquor are a necessity in keeping that monkey off their backs. I observed that these men were always drunk, which was contrary to their ways prior to the crack epidemic. Those who managed to keep their jobs sought intoxication immediately after work each day. Eventually, all lost their jobs, along with their families.

The Bible warns us about the strange woman, as mentioned in this chapter's title, (the strange woman being cocaine), in Proverbs 22: 14 that "The mouth of strange women is a deep pit..." (KJV). Being connected to the crack lifestyle made for a merciless downward spiral whose only end was destruction. As for alcoholism, the Bible says that "Wine is a mocker, strong drink is raging: and whosoever is deceived thereby is not wise." (Proverbs 20: 1—KJV)

I was to find out later that the door of free-base cocaine was to come my way, and soon. The quick increase in the price of marijuana was the avenue by which it came.

# Chapter 20

# The Greater of Two Evils

*"Wherefore come out from among them, and be ye separate, saith the lord, and touch not the unclean thing; and I will receive you." 2nd Corinthians 6:17 (KJV)*

My curiosity as to various means of experimenting with cocaine grew; coupled with the fact that the cost of pot was on the increase. I now see that the dark principality over the drug culture was and is responsible for the manipulation of drug cost, causing the usage of pot to be exchanged for the more powerfully euphoric free base coke.

In 1985 I moved in with Charlton, replacing Logan. They lived in the upstairs of a two family home located near E. Broad and Meadow streets in Richmond. In the beginning it was all a big party. I could hardly remember being sober. Day in and day out, marijuana was the focus of my daily routine. With pot connoisseurs about, the goal was to never run out of smoke. So, "joints" were ever present. Also, on the rare occurrence when I ran out, I kept a stash of reefer roaches (smoked down marijuana cigarettes, which resembled cockroaches), to smoke during hard times.

For those who smoked, our lives were happenless. I routinely came home from work, gathered with friends, immediately began getting high, and watched TV in an almost comatose-like state. Many nights, we didn't sleep, but sat watching HBO, Cinemax, or music videos. We were wasting our years, and were clueless as to the truth.

Prior to moving in with my friends, I began working for an investigative firm, Ranson and Associates, as an undercover operative. I worked undercover at several Richmond area companies during my tenure with the firm. I would write daily reports of my day's experience and give them to my supervisor on a weekly basis. They in turn would present any pertinent information to the various companies' security departments. I reported on such things as employee pilferage, fraudulent cooperate dealings, and drug use.

On occasion, I was given assignments of a covert nature. On one particular case I was sent to Stafford County, Virginia to film a man thought to be malingering, and faking his injury from an accident. The liable insurance company wanted to gain proof that his claim was bogus. So I trekked down to Stafford in my 1974 rusted orange Honda CVCC, with my trusty 8mm camera. There were several hurdles I had to overcome. I didn't have a residential address on the person that I was to stakeout. I went to several area community resources, such as the post office, fire station, and sheriff's department, to secure an address on my subject. Finally, I obtained an address from the sheriff's office. I found the trailer where the man lived, which was several hundred yards into the woods. I was instructed to secure a hiding place and wait to catch the man doing something not conducive to his injury. Do to the heat and rain of that summer's day, I did not follow my boss's directive, and positioned my car in a cover hole. My goal was to catch him bending, lifting, performing yard work, or anything that would expose fraud. My son Jeff called me Inspector Gadget during my tenure with that firm.

Waiting for the subject to arrive, I sat thinking about the cold beer and fat joints of "Sessamia" marijuana to be enjoyed as soon as I got home. I was consumed with the prospect of the euphoria that I was destined to know. Then suddenly, a white pick-up truck quickly blocked me in, with a white man of good size getting out and walking fast toward me. I immediately noticed a shotgun in his rear truck window. Frustrated, he stated that he heard I was looking for him, and wanted to know "what the f...." I wanted. I asked him how he knew that I was looking for him. He exclaimed that his sister was one of the deputy sheriffs for the county, and she alerted him to my inquiry. I instantly received visions of being murdered in those back woods, and a conspiracy would have kept my body from ever being found. Immediately, I considered by relationship with Christ and realized that I was uncertain about my salvation.

Thinking quickly, I told the man I was looking for someone with his same first and last names, but concluded that they had different middle initials. I convinced him that my company sought to repossess a vehicle, but my search had obviously led to the wrong person. In an attempt to sound bold and legitimate, I told the man that I was going to re-examine my information to exempt him, and restart the assignment. I asked him to pardon my mistake, and quickly exited the woods. I thanked God all the way home. I didn't work much longer for the firm, knowing that there would be occasional high risk. The knowledge of my salvation had to be more certain in order for me to continue in that line of work.

Soon after that experience I secured employment as an insurance agent with a company called Bankers Life and

Casualty Company. I worked under a vibrant, young manager named Glen. He helped get me hired and trained me in the various selling techniques profitable for building a clientele. He tried to inspire me to be bold, knowledgeable, tenacious, and even manipulative. I never bought in to the manipulative part. However, I did well my first year under his direction. But Glen dabbled in drugs and heavy drinking, as well as womanizing of a sort. The substance abuse did extend to other agents in the office, but not all. I found myself celebrating with them as a group, or individually, whenever we had good sales. It would always lead us to area bars and grills, getting intoxicated and high. I had advanced from a blue-collar atmosphere to white-collar associations. So, for the first time in my life I began heavy drinking, coupled with chronic pot smoking. But we kept substance abuse secrets from one another. I smoked marijuana, but I thought they only used alcohol. Though I smoked cigarettes and imbibed with them, because I talked Christian, they were uncomfortable with me knowing particulars about their lives while at work and the bar.

After a year with the company, my manager and a fellow associate asked if I smoked pot. I was hesitant to answer, knowing I wanted to be connected within the crowd, but after a few seconds confessed that I had tried drugs. Immediately, my fellow associate pulled out a bag of pot, and Glen produced a pint of home made corn liquor. Within minutes I could hardly think straight. Together, we went to the Casa Grande Restaurant on Midlothian Turnpike, a few miles from our office to get "wasted". Soon after, due to my first year's success, they allowed me to hang out with them. My associate, Tom, and I had on occasion snorted powdered cocaine when we finished a day's work. Tom confessed that he used coke to remain hyped during the day, so to keep the edge in cold calling for sales. He was also quite successful.

Within a year of working for Banker's, I moved out from

the Meadow street house and into my own apartment near Hull Street and Chippenham Parkway. I had received some big checks and bought a 1982 Chrysler New Yorker, within the same time period. But, soon after, everything began to fall apart. Marijuana had always made me lethargic and unmotivated, which made sales nil. I plowed through the next year barely producing any new business, living off of revenues from renewals. My relationship with Glen and other party- goers had weaned to the occasional beer.

My pot smoking was chronic as ever, and I tried desperately to keep this problem from Cathy and my parents. My boss, though equally chronic a user, didn't see my problem, and thought I had betrayed his support as a salesman. But he was having problems on the job, and with family, not realizing that our alcohol and drug use was the cause.

Glen, for a while, continued to keep me on the payroll because he received overrides from my first year's renewal business. Also, he had to keep a certain number of agents in his employ. He did not have the resolve, due to substance abuse, to seek and interview other prospects. This was a time-consuming task, and it only interfered with his partying.

Eventually I moved out of my apartment and moved into my uncle James' house on LaSalle Avenue, located on Richmond's Southside, behind Jefferson village apartments, a project complex. This was drug hell area, and I had fallen into a spiritual and literal death trap. Unknown to me, my uncle had begun a free base cocaine habit, and I was about to succumb to it.

Although I lived at my uncle's home, there was no electricity; for he lived with his girlfriend in another section of Richmond's Southside. James, an auto mechanic, did auto repair in the evenings at his house where he had a two-car garage. He knew how to turn the electricity on when he needed it, but would turn it off at the end of the evening, leaving me to be alone in the dark. I didn't blame him for that because it was a criminal offense, and he wanted to reduce his risk of being caught. I believe the power company eventually took the meter box. I lived there for part of 1987 and 1988.

Gradually my uncle and his friends exposed their free-base use to me, but warned that if I ever tried it, then I would struggle not to become addicted. However, they claimed that they had escaped addiction from the drug.

One particular summer's day, one of my uncles' younger friends came by to get him high on free-base, but my uncle wasn't home. He suggested that if I let him cook his cocaine then he would share it with me. I concurred. For the first time, I smoked cocaine, and it was an extremely powerful hit. I felt dizzy, but of a euphoria that seemed almost spiritual. He allowed me to take a second hit before he left. Within the hour I was hooked! Oh how I should have heeded the word of God that warns us to not touch the unclean thing.

From that very night I began counseling within myself on how to fraudulently and larcenously gain the financial resources for obtaining free base coke. My first goal was to terminate marijuana sources, and find cocaine sources. This would not be a hard task, because some of the pot dealers were fast becoming coke dealers. Many were completely giving up the marijuana trade over the cocaine and/or crack trade. (Crack is cooked up cocaine previously prepared for sale, usually by the dealer, but with other elements for filler to increase the gram weight). Even on the first time of free base use I spent the night "Jones'in" for more cocaine, i.e. having an overwhelming desire for a particular substance, with withdrawal-like symptoms. Before getting to sleep, I occupied my time thinking and conspiring of ways to secure more free-base, while fantasizing about the next feeling of euphoric high. Unknowingly, I began meditating on that drug, which proved to be the doorway to worshiping, that is, giving it a god-like position over my life. I pursued it with all my heart, mind, and strength. But this posture of loyalty is reserved only for the one true God Jehovah, and God is thusly offended. For it is written in the gospel of Mark 12:30, "And thou shalt love the lord thy God with all thy heart, and with all thy soul, and with all thy mind, and with all thy strength: this is the first commandment"(KJV). The Bible says that the Lord our God is a jealous God (Exodus 20:5).

## Chapter 21

# Trick, Trap, Ambush

Sating in my uncle's house, I couldn't stop thinking of this new kind of high. It was as if I had hit the mother load of high experiences. Yet it was as fleeting as a rabbit caught in a vegetable garden and run away by the husbandman. Suddenly, I found myself in a life change, but for the worse. Freebase and crack were more plentiful then pot. It was everywhere in the city, counties, suburbs, and especially the projects throughout the tri-cities area. It became so that it was easier to get coke than any other street drug.

I began doing abominable things in order to get high. At first, I couldn't motivate myself to look for work. Instead, I awaited renewal checks from Banker's Life and Casualty Company that came bi-weekly. My whole focus was on getting that next hit. (Fortunately, I never defrauded an insurance prospect or policyholder during my sales career).

One particular payday I received a $714 paycheck. I was so anticipating of freebasing that I let myself be cheated by my manager. Since I hadn't produced any business in almost a year, he tried to convince me to give him a chunk of that check. He claimed it was due him for keeping me on the payroll. I knew it was blackmail, but my desire to freebase was so strong that I couldn't wait to page my coke dealer. So, I gave in to his demands. He could have sent that check back to the company while claiming that I had been terminated for non- performance. Also, I was guilty of a conspiracy within myself, thinking that as long as I gave him a share of my renewal check then he would allow them to continue without requiring me to stay active. This went on for a while.

With that check, it was the first time I was able to buy abundant cocaine. I beeped my coke dealer, who was one of my previous marijuana sources, named "Tip". I discovered that Tip turned to selling powdered coke for "cook'em up" when witnessing him selling to my uncle and his friends. After rocking up the coke, they began to smoke from their own personal pipes. None wanted to share their glass pipes with one another. The pipe was very precious to them. However my uncle was moved, not by God, to let me smoke from his pipe. He didn't know that his younger friend had already initiated me.

I called Tip and told him that I wanted an eight ball of powder. An eight ball is approximately 31/2 grams of coke. It seemed to take forever to obtain it, but he finally delivered. I had at an earlier time obtained a glass pipe and Charboy copper mesh for smoking. One could buy a test tube from any store that sold a particular kind of cigar which product was packaged in a glass test tube (Satan has truly orchestrated his sorcery to make his wickedness complete in every way). I had all the baking soda I needed to accomplish the cooking process that resulted in rock cocaine.

Alone in my uncle's house, I sat in his hall bathroom cooking cocaine with nervous anticipation. Desperately wanting to hit, I didn't wait for it to rock up. I took a wire hanger, which I used to extract the coke from the glass tube, and allowed the oily substance to drip on the pipe's wiry mesh. Immediately, I took a long, hard hit, and coughed it out. To my disdain, I thought the hit was wasted. However, I did try again, but more slowly and deliberate. Blast off! Take-off accomplished. Never had I experienced such an intense high. Instantly, I became paranoid, checking throughout the house for hidden people while expecting the police to arrive at any moment. But, even with all that paranoia, I had rather risk being arrested then give up the coke. I was a body of fear manifest in the flesh. I was in a state of confusion, with a lost ability to think or speak. I sat in that house, in the dark, wanting nothing but to be left alone with my pipe, paging my dealer throughout the night, until every dollar was gone. I smoked all night.

After running out of freebase, I began scraping the pipe for its white/grayish residue, which proved to be extremely powerful. While light remained on the next day, I found time to look at myself in the mirror. I looked gaunt, dirty, dark, and zombie-like in my countenance. I felt demon-possessed. This was the first time that I despised myself in a big way. I knew that I had exchanged gods, and this god was a baser god. It reminds me of what C.S Lewis writes in his book, The Great Divorce, concerning natural affection, "Brass is mistaken for gold more easily than clay is. And if it finally refuses conversion its corruption will be worse than the corruption of what ye call lower passions. It is a stronger angel, and therefore, when it falls, a fiercer devil." Freebase is that fiercer devil than was marijuana, though both be of Satan.

## Chapter 22

# Mindmeld

*"For as he thinketh in his heart, so Is he"*
*(Proverbs 23:7) KJV*

My obsession with freebasing filled my every waking hour, and even entered into my dream mind when sleeping. Not only were my thoughts of using coke, but also on ways of obtaining it, none of which involved honesty. I knew the Bible says that Satan has come to destroy, kill, and steal from mankind. And that is Satan's objective. This is also the description of his character, i.e. he is not only a liar, but also a thief, murderer, and destroyer. His spirit influenced my mindset. That is, the spirit of sorcery. Everything that Satan exemplifies, I ultimately accomplished. The schemes that I came up with manifested all that lead to Satan's purposes.

My first scheme involved lying to my aunt Shirley. For example, I would tell her that I needed brakes for my car. Tapping into her compassion, she lovingly and generously gave to my cause. I lied to her on occasion, before freebasing, but always feeling remorse. Yet, ravenous for freebase, I felt emotionless and unlived. It was as if I had no soul. It seemed, even then, another ordered my steps, not Christ. This is the essence of witchcraft. That is, Satan or one of his demonic cohorts, usually in cooperation with the flesh (refer to James 1:14), entices to manipulate a willing perpetrator via demonic influence, causing that person to manipulate some unsuspecting, usually kindhearted kin or friend, to commit a fraud or to make an innocent a victim.

Many times, I lied to deceive my aunt, mother (my father wasn't so easily snookered), friends, and my most secretly faithful friend, Cathy.

Week in and week out, my shenanigans became more elaborate. Due to keeping this new-found addiction secret, no one suspected that I was in a death grip. In the beginning it was easy to get money for my habit. Whatever I said to my friends and family was more than acceptable. They knew that I had employment problems, but thought it a phase; and not believing for a moment that it was freebasing or crack addiction. Being blatant, I went to several family members, who remained close, and conversed the same lies, and on the same day. As with the car brakes story, I'd tell them lies, and succeeded in collecting money. I didn't think that they would talk with each other. And in the beginning they didn't. However, gradually they began to sense something was very wrong. So, I backed off for a while and focused on obtaining drugs by earning the money.

Earning money at working odd jobs, helping my uncle James work on cars, in which he often cheated me, hardly satisfied my habit. My uncle found out that I was hooked on coke, and he used me. I worked all day, and he paid as little as $10, while promising he could get me a good hit for that small amount. I never did get any satisfaction. The Bible is true when it says that one reaps what one sows.

I began getting jobs at various restaurant chains in the

Richmond area, usually as a supervisor or manager trainee. But I would lose the job after the first or second paycheck. The two or three hundred dollars that I earned was depleted into pennies within a few hours, even minutes, depending on whether or not I was gipped by buying fake powder.

Nevertheless, my mind fixated on the next hit. So, periodically I'd try obtaining pity from Cathy, asking if I could stay at her new English Hills apartment, located in the far west end of Henrico, County. Aside from my aunt Shirley, I may have defrauded, and definitely stolen more from Cathy then anyone else.

I reminded Cathy that it was winter. She knew I lived in a house with no electricity or heating source. However, unbeknown to her, my uncle had a wood stove in his living room. But, truthfully enough, many nights I was close to freezing. Well, she reasoned that her Christian duty was to help, though we weren't on the best of terms.

Cathy worked night shift for Richmond Memorial Hospital while trying to play mother and father to Jeff, our son. I never helped Cathy with financial support for Jeff. She had all financial responsibility squarely on her shoulders. This is not to downplay Cathy's parents' contribution to Jeff's rearing. They, for the most part, raised Jeff. Regularly, he lived with them for the first twelve years of his life, visiting and living with his mother in spurts.

Waiting for Cathy to go into a deep sleep, I quietly watched TV. I knew that she awakened by 9:45pm for work. Craftily, around 7:00pm, I would take her bankcard from her purse, which she kept on the dinning room table. Unbeknown to her, I once viewed her keying in the pin number while graciously lending me money. I never paid back any money she loaned. (I depended on Cathy's guilt feelings over her secret of another relationship, which devastated me, believing we were engaged. A year earlier, in 1987, I'd given her an engagement ring. I believe this made her give to my pitiful causes. Cathy, at this point, did not know I had a cocaine addiction. This was witchcraft in one of its two most subtle forms. Using ones guilt for gainsaying, and the misuse of a person's trust, as with my aunt Shirley. However, years later, the great goodness of God used both women to show me Godly love, forgiveness, and mercy). Taking her bankcard to an anytime banking machine near Regency Square Mall, I electronically stole, on the average, a hundred dollars per attempt. Sometimes I did these three or four nights in a row. It would be weeks before she found money was missing. She worked so much, sometimes at other hospitals, that her busy and fatiguing schedule made her not mindful to balance her accounts.

I'd proceed to the Southside to locate my cocaine source, monitoring my time allowance all the while. Immediately, upon returning, I would go to the main bathroom and begin cooking. I went undisturbed because Cathy used the half bath in the master bedroom. I couldn't wait for her to go to work. I envisioned obtaining that orgasmic-like euphoria with every blast of the pipe. Once that first puff hit my blood stream, which happened in seconds, I only wanted the pipe. Nothing in heaven or earth was as worthy as freebasing. I only feared Cathy catching me, knowing it would jeopardize my place and time for getting high. Thus, most of the time, with extreme paranoia setting in, I managed to stop smoking long enough to wait out her getting dressed for work. I usually pretended that I was asleep to avoid conversation. This worked because she didn't care to talk to me about anything. I committed this detestable deed periodically over four to six months. But, eventually Cathy would find out and break off all communications with me. She explained that the only reason she didn't have me arrested was because I was Jeff's father. At that time, Jeff showed a deep affection for me, but, in time, that would wean to the recognition that I was his biological father. In spite of all the turmoil due to freebasing, my mind stayed on coke.

Due to losing Cathy again, I resisted using coke for a time. But my inward vow was short-lived. One day, while staring at the walls in my uncle's home, reflecting on the turns my life had taken, there came a knock at the door. A neighbor from down the street, who knew James years earlier during their glamorized drug trafficking years, stood at the door. His name was Ben. He and I, in years to come, would smoke tens of thousands of dollars in crack, to say the least. On the first day, we instantly hit it off. He needed to pick up his girlfriend, whose car had broken down. I, truly, had brake trouble, at this time. My car's brakes had no padding left and it was scraping metal to metal against the car's rotor. But, I did take the risk, and took him. On the next day he came by to thank me. He boldly asked me if I smoked pot, and I said yes. Then he asked if I smoked coke, and I affirmed that also. He proceeded to bring out a test tube with rocked coke in it. We smoked in my uncle's garage. He was generous to me more than with his friend, Starborn, who accompanied him. Ben didn't work at that time, and he only sold marijuana to make small cash. Years earlier, he was a big time dealer, along with my uncle James, but their lifestyle had dwindled away, and freebasing had gripped him, though he consistently denied that he had a coke habit.

Ben, within the hour, had educated me on the various costs of coke in the area. He related that different dealers had diverse prices on coke. I paid as much as $300 per eight ball for powdered coke, but Ben had sources that were closer to king pin status. This allowed him to get an eight ball for as little as $150 per package. This meeting with Ben led to the beginning of chronic use. For years, I alienated myself from previous friends and family. Upon reflection, I had entered into the "twilight zone".

I encountered a subculture, such that, I met people for a

time, as drug dealing acquaintances. Frighteningly, before I knew it, Ben was showing me their gangland style murders reported in the newspapers or on the TV news. Sometimes, the people of this crack culture were found to be the murderers, rather than the murdered. This concerned me the most, because I freaked at the thought of having actual contact with would-be murderers. I wondered how many unsolved murders and attempted murders these men had committed. I shutter at the thought of booking coke, during this early stage, when not knowing these men. I may have become the object of visitation on Memorial Day.

Ben stated that he personally believed that many murders remained unsolved because the murderers were imprisoned on non-related charges. Driving without a license, or being caught dirty with drugs, usually were among the reasons that many violent criminals were arrested. They are jailed for a time, being out of the main stream; thus, the potential for attaching them to more violent crimes becomes cold and remote. Unfortunately, this is the nature of the beast.

From 1987 –1996, I lived the life of an abject liar, cheat, thief, forger, absentee father, deadbeat dad, and one under a form of sorcery, called crack addiction. Again, my thoughts were continually wicked, to do larceny, without regard to the God that chastised me for the previous twenty years, which is manifested in the redemptive work of Jesus Christ. In spite of God's love, this drug-induced witchcraft had caused my mindset to fall into the same mind of the people of Noah's time. They regarded not the grieving of God, or His will for their lives. It is written in **Genesis 6: 5&6** that "… *God saw that the wickedness of man was great in the earth, and that every imagination of the thoughts of his heart was only evil continually. And it repented the Lord that he had made man on the earth, and it grieved him at his heart.*"(KJV)

I thanked the God of heaven and earth that I found grace in His sight. Jesus, can see a far off, and He continually made intercession for me day and night. Truly, I was saved by grace. The Bible says that we are saved by grace through faith. Therefore, God, by His omniscience, imputed future faith He knew would come, while I was yet faithless. Praise God that his mercy truly endureth forever.

# Chapter 23

# ON and ON, and ON

My relationship with Ben grew as we entered into deeper addiction. We became dependent on one another for "get high". Usually it was I who financed our almost daily smoke out.

On one particular day, after receiving one of my inactive paychecks, I went directly to Ben, with the hopes that he could deliver on his promise to get $150 eight balls. I hadn't seen him in almost two weeks since the smoke out in my uncles' garage. I nervously knocked at his door, not knowing if I was about to get ripped off or enter into a promising relationship. Starborn answered the door. Ben's girlfriend, Wanda, was normally at work during the daytime hours. He immediately invited me into the kitchen, where it was better lighted. Ben seemed to intuitively know that I was desirous to score and score big. I wonder if demonic spirits do clue us in when we want to accomplish Satan's work. After all, we were involved with one of Satan's biggest principalities, the black market drug trade, which is only a cog in one of his biggest sorcerous strongholds, drug addiction.

Ben looked at me and said, "How much weight you want?" I indicated that I wanted an eight ball for the price he quoted me two weeks earlier. He tried to convince me that he really charged $200 for the package so to make a profit. I told him that I was willing to make that arrangement. But, he ultimately decided to let me buy for the $150 if I gave him a 50-cent piece (slang for a ? gram of coke). He wanted to smoke coke also, thus, he determined to decrease his risk of getting busted by not making a second drug buy, and better the gram weight by dividing the whole eight ball into four equal parts. To us, this proved to be the better way. I smoked a little with him, and soon left. I could hardly wait to get back to my uncle's house. The covetous desire to smoke coke was overwhelming. I lied to Ben and Starborn by telling them that I wanted to sell the coke. I had packaged the coke into $50 packets. It made me paranoid to think that if I got busted with these packets then I could be given a distribution and possession charge. So, as soon as I returned to James' house, the packages were compiled into one. Upon entering the house I collected the tube, pipe, and baking soda. I meticulously put in all the ingredients, took out my Bic lighter, and cooked the coke. Within minutes I had rock cocaine. I put that hit on the pipe, being very jittery from smoking just minutes earlier at Ben's, and lit up while taking a slow deep breath. Bam! Again, take off. I became very paranoid, and searched the house for hidden police or robbers. Finally, I situated myself in a front side bedroom where I could watch anyone who may come. I could hardly enjoy the moment. It was about then that I saw Ron; another friend of Ben's who showed up while we were smoking. I began to "trip" as to why he was coming to my abode. It seemed as though everything was in slow motion. I couldn't find a place to hide my works, while simultaneously watching him move ever closer toward the house. Finally, I left all the paraphernalia in the bedroom and closed the door. Ron knocked, but I didn't answer. He knocked for what seemed to be a thousand taps at the door. Again, I went in to the bedroom and smoked while he knocked. Eventually, he came to that bedroom window and looked in. I knew that he could not see inside because the room was very dark and had sheer curtains at the window. I could see him, but he couldn't see me. Again, he returned to the front door and knocked harder. I knew he wanted a hit in the worse way. This time I answered. He told me that Ben wanted to book a 50-cent pack (1/2 gram of cocaine) from me. I declined. He persisted in trying to book a package for himself, and again I declined. Lying, I told him that I needed the money right away. Lying is a persistent and necessary part of the drug culture in order for its inhabitants to perpetuate the trade and satisfy the selfish desires of users and dealers alike. I wanted to keep the coke for myself, not being mindful that almost all my money was spent, and made no plans to supply needed items, such as, food, toiletries, laundry items, or gas for the car. For me, the time had come to find another job. My Bankers life gravy train was hastily ending. And all I wanted to do was go on with my pursuit of freebasing.

It seemed Ben and I found a way to get high almost each day. Our whole life centered on developing ways to get cash, or, what we called, "play game", to obtain coke. We would go to extremes, even selling fake powder to other users that wanted small weight. Especially those we knew that wouldn't get too contentious about getting their money back, which wasn't in the realm of possibility when buying off the street. Also, users knew that trying to get a street buy refund was a cardinal sin. It was a life-threatening mistake. Richmond, at that time, was number three in the nation in murders per capita. They were mostly drug related homicides. So, we used that knowledge to scheme on the more timid users. We didn't often use fake powder sales to cheat others, but it was in our arsenal of tricks. Usually, Ben was straight with people for whom he scored. But, many times, I was not given a lot of consideration from Ben when he sold big weight. Many times he would ask me to leave or stay in another part of the house while he smoked with another user. Sometimes he would throw me crumb hits to maintain our smoking relationship. But, as with me, he was more interested in the next hit than equity. Remember, this is a lifestyle of ultimate selfishness. However, I was very hurt and felt slighted. After all, I was Ben's main source of high, and he knew it.

Nevertheless, Ben and I became fast friends. We depended on one another for other things, such as car rides when either of our vehicles was indisposed. We would also talk about the lack of purpose in our lives due to smoking crack, and examine how our lack of motivation and drug use affected our relationships with our families, especially our female counterparts and children. We acted as listeners to one another's sob stories. But we didn't examine the futility of getting off of drugs.

Time seemed to fly. Before long, I had known Ben a year. Dealers came to know us as the two crack heads; fore we had built up a reputation among certain dealers whom we paged, and others that we visited on the streets of Richmond. I was always scoring through Ben. Therefore, drug-bonding relationships not only developed between us, but also with several of the dealers. I would allow them to use my car for drugs, or chauffeured them to their many drop offs. They came to know me as an often buyer, and thus, the possibility for me booking coke became stronger. In the early days many dealers were very discreet to who they booked coke. Murdering a non-payer was becoming commonplace. But the desensitizing to murder by dealers and users was on the rise. Many warned that there would be major consequences or death to pay for not keeping one's word. Thus, some dealers, whom were more interested in money than murder, would give that warning. However, I believe that some dealers, especially the younger pushers, wanted to commit murder. It was becoming a badge of honor. Some juveniles have told me that murdering a person mattered not. They felt that they had not many years to live, coming under the same death curse as their male relatives and friends. Also, many believed that they would only do a few years in a juvenile detention center, being under 18 years of age. They saw where major crimes committed by juveniles carried light consequences; therefore they were more willing to commit crimes than their adult counterparts.

I began booking coke from Tip. At first, I paid on time, mostly out of fear for my life. I built up his trust. But within weeks I began reneging on our agreement, avoiding him like the plague. He usually would wait a day or two before hunting me down. I would hide in my uncle's house when he came looking. My heart would beat like I had just run a mile at full speed. At night I hid my car at the Jefferson Village apartments, a section eight project complex. I'd walk through the woods to my uncle's house, and lie in bed in that dark and cold night. I would eventually find a way to pay him, usually waiting for payday with whatever job I was working. But I felt a foreboding in my spirit.

I came home one day after not paying Tip for a few weeks, and noticed a bullet hole in the front door frame. I can't truthfully say that this hole wasn't there before, but I had never noticed it. Finally, Tip caught up with me, and was surprisingly kind. He wanted to reestablish another payment date, and $10.00 more for the delay. He stated that he was patient because I was James' nephew, but admonished me to pay the money. He also mentioned that his very big friend, who often rode with him, wanted to do me harm because I was "dis'in" his partner. But he forbade him, stating that I bought a lot of coke, and believed that I wasn't "trying to do larceny" against him.

After that close call with Tip, I did convince him to book me another gram at a $100 cost. However, I obtained this coke while unemployed, and without prospects. I enjoyed the entire gram alone, and subsequently went into mental shock. I could not escape the thought that I may be dead in a matter of days! Somehow I managed to obtain $25, probably from Shirley or Cathy, a few days before the whole debt was due. I delivered the money, and hoped he would give me an extension. But, while gladly taking the money, he stated that he desperately needed the remaining balance as per our agreement. He admonished me to pay on time. Well, that scheme didn't work. I was fast losing my mind. I was in need of a miracle. To whom could I turn except the Lord God? I left Tip, went back to my uncle's house and prayed all night. I repented from all my lies, and schemes, and begged God to make a way of escape. I decided to reestablish a salvation relationship with Jesus, asking His forgiveness and restoration. I beseeched His help to get out of debt, and give me another start in life. On the day in which the debt was due, I had no money. I went home to visit my parents and to find a place of peace, but returned to Richmond shortly after. Sitting in James' house waiting for the ultimate show down, I imagined all kinds of ways that I could die. The most prevalent was a shot to the head. However, while I waited for what I thought was my fate, no one showed for a week of nights.

On the beginning of the next week, James stopped by and related that Tip had been busted the previous week, and would do prison time. I knew it was wrong to be happy at the thought of another being jailed, but I was overjoyed. I must say that I found peace in those days prior to Tip getting busted, while waiting to address him. I felt truly saved, and on my way to heaven. And that was every man's final desire, wasn't it? Nevertheless, God had made a way. For the moment, I was free from death's grip. God had delivered, and made for one less street pusher, while giving me another chance to start again. Tip, released some years later, never mentioned the money.

Repentance was short lived, and my crack habit persisted, being the focal point of my existence. All my energies were absorbed in the race to get more coke. It went on and on, day after day.

## Chapter 24

# Deafening the Word

*"He that hath an ear let him hear..." (Revelation 2:7)*

Around the spring of 1989 I began to sense the Lord warning me to stop the life style in which I had entered. He beckoned me to seek Him daily. I was sure of His drawing and recognized His call. Jesus said in the gospels that the sheep hears the voice of the good shepherd. I knew that he was again standing at the door of my heart, knocking! I thanked God that I, at points in my life, worked at developing a relationship with Christ. So, I could tell when the true and living God was drawing near. Was it possible that God would want me now? In spite of all I had done to others and myself, sometimes sinning in the name of the Lord, God called me so that he could embrace me. I felt an inner pulling toward something outward and upward. It was amazing how the love of God imbued me.

I continued to follow the same pattern of substance abuse

as before, but I felt compelled to pray daily, again meditating on the Word of God. It's funny how all consequences seemed to find confirmation in God's Word.

I tried to read and study the scriptures at this time, but found it difficult to concentrate. Why did I lack focus? As a boy I could always center on the Word. I remember seeking relaxation in reading the Gospels while visiting my parents'home, coveting the inner peace and soul stirring it offered. But now, this feeling would not come. Neither did the understanding, which I expected from the scriptures, come. What was happening to me? I couldn't comprehend even the simplest of context. To the contrary, I sensed a struggle going on within me that pitted me, in my spirit, against the truth of the Gospel. I sensed that within me was another spirit that couldn't receive the Word of God. It was as if my inward self was a magnet that repelled the magnet of God's beckoning. Two magnets, if positioned wrongly, will repel one another. I knew that God's Word was calling to my soul, but my soul had a barrier between it and God's Word and, more specifically, His deliverance Word. That barrier was that the copulation of my spirit had become one with an unholy spirit, i.e. a spirit of sorcery, which was manifested in a crack cocaine addiction. I was willing at this time to give up all substance abuse, including alcohol and cigarettes. I coveted it so that I wept much for deliverance. Nevertheless, I found it impossible to gain. Jesus states in Matthew 26:41 that *".... the spirit indeed is willing, but the flesh is weak"(KJV)*. Although the barrier to my receiving understanding from the Word was due to an addiction spirit, it was yet operating through my flesh. The pleasure centers of my fleshly mind yearned for that euphoria afforded it via freebase or crack. It was this way with marijuana, but pot didn't have a lasting negative effect on my ability, as I weaned myself from it, to receive God's Word when I sought it. But, crack cocaine is a more powerful demon.

Indeed, there existed a blockage between the Word of God and my receiving it. The Bible explains why such hindrance occurs. I was operating not only with a spirit of addiction, but also in the nature of the flesh. Follow me as the Spirit leads us through the understanding of this matter. First, it is written in James 1: 14 that *".... every man is tempted, when he is drawn away of his own lust, and enticed"(KJV).* There exist enticements to the flesh, and, by implication, there must exist an enticer, i.e. one that will provoke another to give in to temptation. This is, in the case of substance abuse, devil spirits that have the ability to affect our mental processes (these devil spirits can not only work independently, but sometimes have as hosts or vessels drug dealers and users). Can Satan influence our thoughts? Yes! Jesus teaches in the parable of the sower of the seeds found in the Gospel of Mark 4:15 that Satan has the power to snatch the Word of God from our hearts, i.e. from our understanding or memory. Therefore, devils can divert our thinking, particularly if we are not grounded and rooted in the Word, prayer, and walking in obedience to God's will.

These enticements and enticers operate in various ways. For example, while either visiting my son Jeff at his mother's apartment or my parents home, I might be reading, looking at TV, or sitting with my grandmother, who suffered from Alzheimer's, and without any warning, I'd get an overwhelming desire for crack. This came from nowhere, and hit like a ton of bricks. Bam! It was as if an onslaught had come upon me, and I was overthrown without a battle. My thoughts and movements were ordered by a compelling to find and secure crack. Some may say these were simply withdrawal symptoms. But I didn't experience the shakes, sweating, or confusion. I simply wanted to pursue the possessing of crack with all tenaciousness. It seemed as if I was under the control of another entity, not Christ. Besides, who's to say that even withdrawal symptoms of a substance abuser aren't initiated from spiritual beings moving and operating among men? Can devils really affect a person in such a gross manner? Yes! We read in the gospels that Jesus cast out devils that possessed men. The possession occurred by the spirit(s) literally entering into the mind or body of the possessed person. A very real demonic spirit had entered into the brain of the person under its control. Demonic possession, according to the scriptures, can even afflict a person's physical health. Jesus speaks of how Satan has bound some with physical malady. But, thank God that Christ can deliver us out of them all (Psalm 34:19), AMEN!

The notion of spiritual principalities is also explained in the book of Ephesians chapter six and verse 12. At this time in my life was I possessed? I can't tell. But, at the very least, I was most certainly oppressed by demonic influences.

Enticers come also by way of our flesh nature, such as with our eyes, which have its own potential for lust (1st John 2:16), our smell and taste, which, for me, was part of my experience during euphoric recall. All of which plays a part in the drug abuse experience. For example, while traveling Midlothian Turnpike in Southside, Richmond, I would often ride past known drug dealers waiting for the Greater Richmond Transit buses. Because I had become well known, they would inadvertently yell for me to stop. Instantly, I would feel that nervous anticipatory feeling that surfaced shortly before I obtained crack cocaine. Immediately, I would make a "U" turn in response to their beckoning. The sight of the gram weight, smell, and taste of the coke prompted me to extend myself in not only taking the drug dealer wherever he pleased, but to enter into territories that I wouldn't, at that stage in my addiction, normally go. I ventured with the dealer into places such as Hillside Court and Afton apartments, which were known drug strongholds, and oftentimes places of homicide investigations.

*How* did operating in the flesh nature and my fleshly mind, hinder my reception of the Word of God? Well, the apostle Paul writes in 1st Corinthians 2:14 that *"...the natural man receiveth not the things of the Spirit of God...neither can he know them, because they are spiritually discerned."(KJV)* And we know that God is not separated from his Word. As it is written in St. John 1:1 that *"...the word was God"(KJV).*

Why could I not receive this kind of spiritual discernment? Because it is required that one is of the right kind of spirit. Paul continues to explain in verse 11 of 1st Corinthians chapter 12 that *"...the things of God knoweth no man, but the Spirit of God".* And reading up to verse 10, Paul states that *"God hath revealed them unto us by his Spirit: for the Spirit searcheth all things, yea, the deep things of God."* The Holy Spirit must reveal the Word of God to the believer, for without Him there *is* no revelation. Paul teaches us in the epistle to the Romans 8:16 that *"The Spirit itself beareth witness to our spirit...." (KJV).* So, this is the essence of the hindrance that left me wanting, that is, the spirit that directed me was not the Holy Spirit. But I gave way to another spirit to lead my thinking. That is why I was able to discern the things of the demonic princes of darkness reigning in the drug culture.

But God did not leave me hopeless. God beckoned me in my spirit to pray and receive the lordship and restoration of Jesus Christ.

There *is* a drawing toward Christ that is initiated by God. This pull toward Jesus is put on any non-believer (including any backslider), by way of God's omniscience, and omnipotence, to come under the redemptive work of Christ at Calvary's cross, in spite of that person's inability to comprehend the Word of God. Thus, God went back to His first touch on my life by calling me to repentance, to seek His face in prayer; and making me mindful of rudimentary scripture, which the Holy Spirit brought back to my memory. I am truly thankful that my parents allowed some Word to be sown into me as a youth, and for God compelling me to study privately. And, in regards to God again initializing the coming together of a relationship with Christ, Jesus says in John 6:44 that *"No man can come to me, except the Father which hath sent me draw him...." (KJV)*

God went back and did the first works, as he would a non-believer who has yet to believe. I thank God for His grace and mercies.

Truly, I heard the voice of the good shepherd. I had prayed often, and my drug use was dramatically reduced as far as clean days. However, the crack smoking had not completely gone. I would pray and repent almost daily, periodically backsliding. And when I backslid I did it big time. I participated in smoking all-nighters, booking coke, and being up for days in a row. I was not mindful of the scriptures that Jesus taught in Luke 11: 24-26 when he says that spirits will return to men after leaving them for a time. And again Jesus taught that some spirits come out but by prayer and fasting (refer to Matthew 17:21). All I knew was that I needed more. There was a bonifide war between the flesh and the spirit, and between the Holy Spirit and demonic spirits who were desirous of my soul. The Holy Spirit does not force itself on any man; yet, He will call one to *willingly* submit himself to Him. This is not so with demonic entities. Also, a pivotal variable in this wrestling match was my free will, in which existed a struggle between the will of my flesh and the will of my spirit. The Bible says that the spirit wars against the flesh, and they work contrary one to the other (Galatians 5:17). But, God is faithful. In my spiritual hearing I sensed that God was leading me to a place of power, and He did. One night as I was driving through Charles City Co., I felt a tug at my heart to go to Bible study at Elam Baptist Church. It was Spring of 1989, a Thursday night. I dared to enter into the study session that night, and found as the teacher, a former schoolmate, Dale Wallace, who aspired to the ministry of Jesus Christ. This day changed my life forever. I had never heard anyone teach in such a bold, charismatic, yet, humble manner. He taught with authority and a Pentecostal bent. I somehow knew that God wanted me to confess to Dale my drug addiction. The Bible says that we are to confess our strongholds to each other. Consequently, he and his wife went into battle mode. After everyone in the class left for the night, we stayed behind for prayer. They bound and rebuked drug spirits from my mind and body, beseeching the Lord for complete deliverance. Also, Dale blessed me with 30 minutes of fruitful counseling after prayer warring. It is of a truth when James 5:16 admonishes to *"Confess your faults one to another, and pray one for another, that ye may be healed. The effectual fervent prayer of a righteous man availeth much"(KJV).*

## Chapter 25

# The Teaching of Godly Truth Through Godly Men

*"Study to shew thyself approved unto God" (KJV)*

Dale was the first person that I personally knew with a bold profession in his walk of faith. I'd seen ministers on TV that expressed their faith in a similar way. Also, in that time, I visited a church in which the pastor showed a bold posture in believing the Word of God, and manifesting the gifts of the Holy Spirit. That man was Pastor Steve Parsons of the Richmond Christian Center. I was very impressed with his teaching and grasp of biblical truth. He preached and taught a deeper truth than I had ever heard from any sermon in which I personally attended. However, I did not stay with his ministry. But, on the day that I entered into the teaching of my old school mate, I entered into teaching desperately needed. It was as if I was hearing truth that had a lasting effect on my heart and mind, as it empowered and trained me to fight spiritual battles. Again, the Word was coming alive within me. I sensed a kindling of fire sparks. This moving of the living Word was definite in its operation. I understood better the scriptures, and felt more confident that God wanted us, that is, all believers, to be on the ready to be used as His vessels, for His purposes at His will and to His glory. Also, I sensed a renewed call to preach.

About the time that I attended Elam Baptist Bible study, I moved home with my parents. Not working, and feeling a fresh move of God in my life, I moved from my uncles' abandoned house. For a while, I diligently attended bible study. But, old ways and old friends began resurfacing. So, I wavered in my faith while not knowing exactly why I was unable to restrain myself from these periodic overwhelming desires to use crack. Dale had shared with me that which Jesus spoke in the Gospel of St. Luke 11:24-26, which discusses that when the unclean spirit comes out of a man, it will ultimately return. However, I didn't understand why this desire kept coming. Was I not delivered? Had not the spirits been rebuked? Why did God let them return? Did not God's Word say that He would not let any temptation come upon me that I could not bare? Is God's Word true? These were some of the plethora of questions that continued to bombard my thinking. There seemed to be a growing panic within me. Entertaining thoughts of doom, I thought my salvation was lost, never to be obtained again.

I held on to what little hope I could muster from scriptures that justified trusting God. In spite of what I, a mere man, couldn't do or comprehend, I continued to beseech Jesus for help, though I became unsure if He would.

As I struggled with periodic crack use, and keeping the

Word of God in obedience, I was lead to listen to various radio shows and ministries. In the beginning, oddly enough, I felt compelled to listen to the Rush Limbaugh program, on 1140am radio in Richmond. At first, I thought he was a loud mouth, arrogant, white racist. I say *white* racist because I have known of some *black* racists. I must say that within a few minutes of hearing, I discerned that he was not racist. Also, after a few more days of listening I could tell that he was neither loud-mouthed nor arrogant, but, rather, he was bold and confident. I determined confident because he found confidence in the truth. When a man knows the truth of a matter, and stands in that truth, then he will have confidence and increase in his confidence as long as he stands in the truth. The apostle Paul writes in the epistle to the Ephesians that when one has done all that they can to stand on their principles, then, in spite of the appearance of negative circumstances, they must continue to stand. Each time that I attempted to turn the radio knob, I sensed a moving to listen. What did this have to do with my faith walk with Christ? Why should I think that I could get spiritual truth from a man that didn't teach and speak the Word of God? Or did he? As I listened to his program he talked about taking personal responsibility for our own lives, trusting not in government, but in one's God given ability and in God Himself. He proclaimed that setting goals for oneself and embarking on achieving those goals *is* the essence of success. Somehow, I sensed that there was an automatic implication that his encouragement called for a beseeching of God to bless our endeavors. I found it strange that as I listened to his verbiage, and filtered it through my mind, God was filling in gaps in my thinking; blending Rush's words with the scriptures. For example, I heard Rush talk about how it is necessary for a person to have the right perspective about themselves as they pursue their purpose in life. He was speaking from a point of view that denounced how the government was instrumental, by many of its social programs and its entitlement seeking culture, in fostering low self esteem, as one of several byproducts of this welfare induced vicious cycle of dependency. (Note: this is not to say that all social programs are not expedient, many are essential). I remembered how God's Word expresses that as a man thinketh in his heart so is he (Proverbs 23:7), and again it is written in Romans 12:2 that we are not to be conformed to this world system, but be transformed by the renewing of our mind. A change to the *right* perspective can change a person's life. As time went on, I saw many correlations between Rush's socio/political positions and the Word of God. Though he may not count himself a minister by man's standards, but he ministered truth to my soul, and God showed me how Rush's speaking was consistent with His edicts. Maybe he did have talent on loan from God. (I continue to get necessary information from his program, which exposes the truth of men's deeds whether they are honest and prudent, or deceptive and self-serving. Although he speaks from a social and political perspective, he is also exposing wickedness in high places) Ephesians 6:12.

Rush's show was only the beginning of other radio broadcasts on which I focused. Also, these shows came to my attention by my faithful friend, Cathy.

It is interesting how Cathy and I kept linking up. In the Spring of 1989 our son Jeff became very sick. He stayed with me at my mother's house for a time, so that I could care for him while Cathy worked. After two weeks, Cathy came to visit. She and I talked about our life's situations, Jeff and our past. I explained my entering into an edifying bible study, and that it was teaching me so many things about how God entered into the affairs of men. She told me that she had been praying that God would show her, and bless her with a Godly man. I didn't claim to be that man, but I desired greatly to become him. Cathy, at this time, was very much involved with another. I didn't know what to do about my feelings toward her. But, God knew the end from the beginning. Eventually, Cathy and I began going to bible study together, which helped to restore our relationship. We sought to develop our new relationship according to the Word of God. Approximately one year later, we were married.

While Cathy and I worked on fostering a harmonious relationship, we began doing many things, such as shopping and riding to work together. As we traveled, we discovered many radio ministries that were fruitful for us. We began listening to such broadcast as "Turning point" with Dr. David Jeremiah, after whom my wife, sort of, name our son- Jeremiah David; and the "Focus on the family" radiobroadcast, with Dr. James Dobson. These ministries caused us to become ravenous for the Word of God.

Another pastor to whom we often listened was Pastor Charles Evans of Temple Avenue Baptist Church, in Colonial Heights Virginia. We sometimes called into his radio ministry, seeking answers to bible questions. In addition to these mainstay programs, we also discovered ministries of such people as Tony Evans, Charles Stanley, Dr. J. Vernon McGee's taped radio teachings, Adrian Rodgers, Bishop Wellington Boone and Joyce Myers, to mention a few. Also, we found several TV ministries that helped us to understand today's issues that plagued our nation, *and* our personal lives. They included the "700 Club" with Pat Robinson, the televised Billy Graham crusades, and the "Old Time Gospel Hour" with the Rev. Jerry Falwell, whom we have met, and found to have a sweet and kind spirit. *We continue to follow these ministries today, as they follow the truth of the Word of God.* Also, along with these long-standing ministries, we have discovered more broadcasts that powerfully teach the Bible. These include such ministers as Bishop B. Courtney McBath of Calvary Revival Church in Norfolk, VA; Ravi Zacharias, whom is a Christian apologist;

Dr. Erwin Lutzer of Moody Church, and Dr. Michael Youssef of the "Leading The Way" ministry. We received books and literature, which these ministers and their ministries produce. Why do I mention some of these flourishing Christian ministries? God *has* called a great cloud of witnesses to preach and teach the scriptures mightily in this present time. And we as citizens of the United States of America *are* without excuse as to why we are not walking in the truth and obedience of God's Word. The Word of truth is being shouted from the mountaintops. Yet, as a nation, we reject the witnesses that God has sent. And God has taken this excuse away, which many might claim, that is, they have not heard the Word of God. However, God's plan for me was that I might be filled with His truth, proclaimed by men and women of God, set up in this nation to boldly proclaim His truth, and expose the deceptions of the enemy, Satan. I was truly built up in the Lord. But sadly, this crack addiction would rear its ugly head again!

## Chapter 26

# The Revisiting of Old Friends, Old Places, Old Habits

*"Blessed is the man that walketh not in the*
*Counsel of the ungodly" (Psalm 1:1)*

After a time of being clean and growing in the Lord, I desired to visit my old acquaintance, Ben. For a while I resisted, but that resolve was short-lived. The temptation was not Ben himself, but rather that which he represented. In him, I had a place to smoke crack, and a person to take the risk of buying the rocked drug. He risked his life, in that, he was used as the middle man in a great many drug purchases, taking most of the risks of getting busted, stuck up, beat up, or killed. On several occasions he was robbed and at risk of being shot. We, who depended on him to play the middleman, didn't realize the chances he took to get us high. However, Ben required that he be reciprocated for his connections and risks. Usually, most buyers gave him product as pay for making the deal. I routinely shared up to half of my product with him to show some gratitude for his hospitality. I find it rather ironic that we showed gratitude for a thing that merely made us Satan's pawns in his heinous and twisted drug-induced menagerie. This drug world held many wicked deeds as part of its make-up, including killings, drug addictions, sexual immorality, perversion, larceny, betrayal, lyings, thieveries, and con games. Many of us committed these kinds of acts, having done all in the name of crack. If I were judged for every time I purchased and used illegal drugs, my sentence would have been for thousands of years. Now I am truly grateful for God's mercy toward me, who was the chief of sinners.

Not knowing that I would sink back into the cesspool of addiction, I visited Ben and other old drug partners and dealers. Again, I gave up the delight that I experienced in the Lord, and reconnected myself to the pleasures of sin. I hoped that it would be a pleasure enjoyed but for a short season. However, it would continue to be the stronghold it had proven to be for years.

On this drug junket, I made some other friends who came from more family-oriented and church backgrounds. They were men not brought up on the city streets of Richmond, and seemed not knowledgeable of the wickedness of their chosen lifestyles. We became so used to smoking crack together, that we knew of each other's payday. We planned who would buy the next high based on a previously planned agreement. But these agreements were rarely adhered to. Nevertheless, we became smoking buddies, getting together on Thursday and Friday nights at Ben's.

We all suffered family tribulations resulting from our alcohol and substance abuse, and became each other's counselors and advisors. A "click" developed within our drug

circles, though rarely did we know one another's real or sur-
names. Nicknames were all that were required. No one
really wanted whole names known, for it was part of the protection we coveted in case lying, stealing, or larceny
occurred within the click. Along with Ben and myself, there
were "Big Man", Martin, Frog, Harry and a few others
whose names I either can't remember or never knew. We
would give advice as to how to manipulate our wives, drug
dealers, and employers in the hopes of not losing our jobs or
families. None of us wanted to walk in contradiction to
God's will for our lives, yet, our ways were unholy at their
core. We submitted ourselves to the ways and influences of
Satan's devices, notwithstanding our good intentions, such
that, all that we thought and did was ungodly. Thus, none of
our counsels were profitable. Of the group, only Ben and I
remained married, with much domestic dysfunction; and
none of us retained our jobs. I lacked the ability to compare
the kinds of fruit reaped from my different walks, that is, my
walk in the ways of the Lord, and my walk in the ways of
the enemy. During clean times, with God's help, I restrained
myself from drugs; and enjoyed good marital success and
prosperity. Yet, when I backslid, all the good fruit that I
enjoyed turned rotten, or slipped away. Ah! God's Word is
true when it teaches, in **Psalm 1:1-6**, *"Blessed is the man
that walketh not in the counsel off the ungodly, nor
standeth in the way of sinners, nor sitteth in the seat of the
scornful. But his delight is in the law of the Lord; and in
his law doth he meditate day and night. And he shall be
like a tree planted by the rivers of water, that bringeth forth
his fruit in his season....and whatsoever he doeth shall
prosper. The ungodly are not so: but are like the chaff
which the wind driveth away... For the Lord knoweth the
way of the righteous: but the way of the ungodly shall perish"*(KJV).

## Chapter 27

# "Am I My Brother's Keeper?"

*God's empowerment of men—The ministry of "The House of Life" (Brother's Keepers Ministries, Inc.)*

As I dove headlong into the familiar drug world, I became desperate for help. After a year of being married, I decided to enter into a residential drug treatment program. It was St. John's drug rehabilitation program, located in western Henrico County on River Road. It was a 30-day program, which was mostly paid for by my wife's major medical insurance. I found the program a viable escape from the perpetual drug chase that I participated in daily. However, I was uncomfortable with attempts they made to rehabilitate me. I was told that there was no healing from drug addiction, and that I would be an addict for the rest of my life. Yet, I knew within the depths of my heart, that there *is* nothing too hard for the Lord. I was told that I could change my lifestyle, and make a commitment to change my ways. But I would never be able to do drugs without it causing dire effects on my life and relationships — this was an accurate assessment. Although their counsel on the consequences of substance abuse were correct, the belief that there is not healing, but only a state of continuing recovery, was false. Somehow, in my heart, I knew the truth of God's healing power, but had a hard time verbalizing it. Also, getting people to agree with me, I felt, were fruitless. So, I didn't try. I tried to glean from the program, but, aside from some nutritional benefits, time away from the drug culture, and recreational time, I sensed not the truth of what God would have me to know in regards to being loosed from drug addiction. I was told by psychologists and wellness counselors that I could regain my life if I followed the twelve-step program. I realized that there were some benefits within the twelve steps, such as confessing that I was powerless to manage my own life. But, it didn't allow me to believe that I could be healed and empowered by God to enjoy victory over the stronghold of substance abuse. It was clear that they believed one could live a life of being clean from drugs, but never loosed and healed from the predisposition of alcohol and drug addiction. However, it is written in 2nd Corinthians 5:17 that *".... if any man be in Christ, he is a new creature: old things are passed away; behold, all things are become new"(KJV).*

Another faulty concept of the twelve- step program was the encouragements to connect to one's higher power, that is, the god of our understanding. I observed in meetings that different people had different gods in which they worshipped, and proclaimed that their gods were beneficial to help manage addiction. And we were instructed to respect and lift up one another in our attempt to connect to our higher power, regardless of whoever or whatever it was.

This was spiritually dangerous to me. The Bible says that we are not to lean to our own understanding, but acknowledge the one true and living God (Proverb 3:5-7). And again, it is written that apart from Jesus Christ, there is no true deliverance.

I sensed that God was not pleased with me encouraging people to follow false gods. I studied and prayed unto Jesus Christ nightly before bedtime, and I felt confident in the Lord, though I sensed a spirit of confusion creeping in and clouding my knowledge of the scriptures. I sensed that it had something to do with being subject to the ranting of others claiming beliefs that I knew were contrary to Bible truth. Seeds were being sown into my spirit that didn't jive with God's Word, or with his Spirit. There were other spirits afoot. For example, there may have been some that worshiped the spirits of their loving parents or grandparents (any true experience in this case would have been deception fostered by spirit guides and/or familiar spirits—which are demonic spirits of deception and wicked influence). Also, some may have professed Buddhism and practiced yoga, encompassing a form of channeling. One man even stated that he considered his higher power to be a doorknob, and that it was profitable for him to have faith in it. That particular man, some time later, committed suicide. Consequently, all those with whom I came in contact, after leaving the program, went back into active addiction, including myself. The Bible teaches that it is required that we receive power to fight the good fight of faith in order to gain victory over strongholds, and dark drug principalities are no exception. The recidivism rate for drug recovery participants is very high. It has been said that only three percent of drug rehab participants remain permanently clean. Ninety-seven percent fall back into the death grip of Satan's devices. But God did not leave me nor forsake me. He presented a way of escape out of my addiction dilemma.

After years of continual using, attending Narcotics Anonymous, and seeing a professional drug counselor, I believed that I was running out of possible help systems.

My wife, in her attempt to find counseling as a co-dependent, contacted a Christian family and marriage counselor named Margaret Duke. A small-framed woman, she seemed to be bold and full of fire. She convinced Cathy to encourage me to see her as a couple, and I complied. Margaret talked with us during that first meeting, but made some inquiries that I didn't want revealed to Cathy, thus requesting that we speak with her separately. After listening to each of us, she discerned that I needed a vigorous residential Christian drug program. Margaret referred me to a man by the name of Reverend Ray Smith, a member of the Richmond Christian Center. Rev. Smith had opened a drug ministry called "Brother's Keepers Ministries" located in a newly renovated building called the "House of life". This building once housed a funeral home. I immediately notified Rev. Smith, but did not respond to his admonition to let him interview me as a possible candidate for his program. He also encouraged me to come to the ministry's daily and weekly teachings and meetings. Though I felt compelled, I recoiled. However, about a year later I was at my wits end, separated from my wife and children, who, within those years since leaving St. John's, had come to be born. My beautiful and very special children were ever on my mind. Born in order of their names, Jeremiah, Jacquelyn (called Jackie), and Jasmine, all showed great affection for me, and were patient in their hopes that their mom and I would again be together. I wanted so much to live the life of the Word that seemed to continue to burn within me. I can't quite explain why I felt compelled to pray and study the Bible, as well as various writings of Bible scholars. After all, I was as enslaved to the drug culture as always. So, where was this appetite to consume God coming from? All that I could think of was that the Bible says that

God knows the end from the beginning. Did God know something about me that I didn't know about myself?

I'm sure God was using my aunt Shirley to guide me in my life's choices. She often times would minister to me about the will of God for my life as a husband, father, and servant of Christ. She always seasoned her words with salt. She allowed me to stay at her home in South Richmond for a long time, while I struggled with my drug addiction. She never let on that she suspected my addiction to be as chronic as it truly was. But she seemed to know I needed her time and her space to let God work within me. And her loving care was beneficial for my soul. I finally came to the decision that I must seek vigorous and powerful help in order to find complete and permanent deliverance from all substance abuse. I decided to call Rev. Smith at the House of Life.

Upon my calling Rev. Smith, I had decided that I would go for broke and become sold out for Christ. I committed myself to doing whatever it took to be restored to Christ and my family. Rev. Smith asked Cathy and me to come for a meeting. We met with him at the appointed time, and found him to be quite matter-of-fact about the need for me to be certain of my commitment to come under the Brother's Keepers Ministry. He listened very intently to my story of addiction. I expressed that I had been drug free for over a month at that point and had been fasting, studying the word of God, and praying diligently during that time. I told him how I sensed that the word of God and the presence of God, as it were, were busting out from within me. I felt like I was going to explode with life, and as a rushing mighty river of pure water. I needed a catalyst to help this eminent explosion find perspective, and to direct its flow. Also, I believed that God wanted me to enter into that ministry, though, within myself, I felt that I had finally kicked the crack habit, as many times before. In my spirit, I knew that I was to receive from the House of life things of God that were not available at twelve- step oriented drug rehabs. I sensed that I was destined to learn Godly things and gain new perspectives that I, as of that time in my life, had never realized or been taught before. And I was not disappointed. I entered the House of life under a ninety-day commitment to endure the entire program.

My first day, I was greeted at the main entrance by the Reverend James Perry. Dr. Perry was a family, marital, and substance abuse counselor at the House of Life. He, as well as the other ministers, was very sound in the faith. Dr. Perry taught from anywhere in the scriptures, but mostly Proverbs. I found him to be wise in the scriptures, and able to relate the Word of God directly to our marital, occupational, and spiritual plights. He helped us to see clear causes and effects of our wayward decisions, according to the scriptures. He brought out perspectives that seemed to be common sense, yet, not grasped by any present. Reverend Perry admonished us to always examine our love walk with Christ.

Next, I met minister Martinez, who spoke much on the detrimental effects of drugs. He reminded us that Satan is ever ready to take up lordship in our lives. Thus, we must be sober, diligent, and watch for his deceptive devices.

I later encountered Minister Alvin Boyd who taught much on biblical marital standards. Also, he taught on God's perspectives concerning family and parent/child relationships. Minister Boyd showed us the effects of generational curses on families, and how they were perpetuated from generation to generation. He taught on God's plan for being loosed from curses, such that, the sins of the father did *not* have to fall upon the son. He, as well as the other ministers, emphasized how Jesus is the great Liberator of all in bondage to sin, if He is sought.

There were other well-versed and Spirit-filled ministers who played important roles in our faith growth and empowerment. However, there were none quite like Reverend

Harold Luster. This man of God was like no man I've ever met. He made his home at the House of Life, and committed himself to living with the men at the residential program. It intimidated me that he made such a commitment. But when I listened to his teachings, it seemed like we were hearing one of the prophets of old. He taught us to listen to the voice of God, and submit to the Holy Spirit for spiritual empowerment, through prayer, intense Bible study, and practicing lifelong faithfulness to God. Rev. Luster also educated us on the gifts of the Holy Spirit, and how to discern and use one's gift(s) within and without the body of Christ, to the glory of God. He also stressed that we, as delivered and committed men of God, should always walk as men of God ought to walk—with integrity, humility, meekness, and boldness, but not prideful, haughty, or arrogant. He was a no-nonsense teacher. He insisted that our ninety-day stay was a kind of basic training for the spiritual warfare that we would incur the rest of our lives. We were to be the Christian warriors for our families and communities, as well as our own recurring battles. He showed us how to wear the whole armor of God, and admonished us to never take it off. At times, he was gruff in his way, but there were never a doubt of the agape love that abided within him. He exemplified that true warrior spirit, mixed with a firm grasp of the Word of God, which is the sword of the Spirit.

Finally, there was the executive director and visionary of the Brothers Keepers Ministries, the Reverend Ray Smith. He seemed to bring together all that the other ministers taught. Rev. Smith gave us the big picture of how our learning would come together victoriously in Christ. I saw that Rev. Smith was filled with compassion, vision, and Godly counsel, and was confident in his calling as head of this ministry. With Christ-like patience and purpose, he looked beyond our faults and saw our needs. Oh! How wonderful and varied are God's manifold blessings.

I must also credit Pastor Steve Parsons for his insight into the ways of God, which he taught twice each Sunday at the Richmond Christian Center. Wherever there may have been gaps in our syllabus of lessons at the House of Life, Pastor Parsons most certainly, in our hearing, filled in those gaps on Sundays.

I was indeed overwhelmed by the power, commitment, dedication, knowledge, and sacrifice of these men of God. I'd never met men with such a calling on their lives. Spirit-filled and gifted disciples of Jesus Christ they were. It concerned me that I may not be able to live up to their Godly examples. But I left there confident in the Lord, restored in my marriage, and to Christ. In Christ, I had vision for my life and family. I wrote down my visions, goal by goal, and step by step as is suggested in the book of Habakkuk 2:2-3. I decided on a total of five long and short-term visions, and ultimately, in Christ, I accomplished them all.

## Chapter 28

# Death Covenant

*"Wilt thou lay down thy life for my sake?" (John 13:38)*

I left the House of life full of vigor and self-expectation, believing that my drugging days were over. I had studied the Word of God like there was no tomorrow. Fasting and praying fervently, I was renewed in God's call to preach. Also, I attended after-care meetings for many months. There even came opportunities to counsel and minister to others of the deliverance power of God. I was filled with the living Word, and the joy of the Lord was my strength. Burning with fire in my spirit, I believed that I was sold out to Christ. Periodically, I experienced several strong temptations to use crack, marijuana, and alcohol, successfully bringing each wayward thought into captivity unto the obedience of Jesus Christ (2nd Corinthians 10:5). My marriage was surged with vigor and promise. My children were full of life, joy and glow. All was well with my house. But, at some point within that first year of post Brother's Keepers Ministry, I became weak to the onslaught that sporadically came my way. This time around, the return to crack made my whole life fall into dysfunction. My wife insisted that I leave the house, my jobs were suddenly in jeopardy, and my children seemed to lose that glow which they illuminated daily. Twice, our eldest son Jeff threatened to fight me. I couldn't even find the wherewithal to visit Sunday school, which I loved attending. Seeking the Lord's intervention and strength, I repented daily of this drug related sorcery. Yet, I fell again and again.

My wife allowed me to stay at home. But this was due mostly to my refusal to leave the children. I didn't fear separation from my household, because I knew that my place was with my family, although I gradually abdicated my position of father over to my wife, again! What was I to do? My heart was for Christ. Yet, I continued to fall into the sin of substance abuse. I knew that Christ had delivered me, but I kept falling. What was missing in the great scheme of things? What was the common denominator in my *failing* faith walk? Again, I was at my wits end.

One afternoon, while contemplating my spiritual plight, I sensed a need to contact Rev. Ray Smith. My wife had mentioned that I desperately needed to talk with him, and soon. Nevertheless, I put the call on hold, not suspecting the delay meant that my very life would be at risk.

I lived for several months out of the will of God, smoking more crack than ever. The consequences were close to becoming lethal. My first close call with death was in the winter season following the year after leaving the House of life. One night, at about 1:00 am, I found myself searching for crack at the dark and dimly lit Afton apartments in South Richmond. Throughout the past 15 years there had been numerous murders reported on their very grounds, with many unsolved. I knew these facts, but the drive within me to use was overwhelming. Two young boys, approximately 14 years old, approached my red compact wagon, and asked what I was looking to score. I requested a $10 rock. At that time of night only small time local youths were out, thus, small buys were normal. As I waited for one of the young boys to gather his package of coke, the other kept telling him to "do it, do it", meaning, to shoot me. But I was not completely attentive to what he really meant. Then suddenly, the same boy who spoke to his friend took over the dealings and produced a gun, which I vaguely saw in the under arm of the boy who pretended to have coke. They put the gun to my head and demanded all the money. I gave them my wallet as the gunman reached into the car and searched my pockets. I had more cash but they didn't find it. I foolishly insisted that I had no other monies. I wanted to maintain some funds for another attempt at finding crack. I wasn't afraid, as I should have been, but was only concerned about my next hit. One of the boys wanted to shoot me, but they seemed confused as to whether or not to go through with it. Finally the gunman said for me to leave and never return. This directive from the mouth of the perpetrator was most definitely a warning and reprieve from God, but I ignored the obvious. Upon my escape from danger, I trekked to nearby Hillside Court apartments, where I pursued that anticipated hit of crack for which I almost gave up my life. I finally scored a tiny rock of coke with the $10 the thieves didn't find. I immediately lit up, but received no rush from the hit. It was a complete waste in every way. For most of the last stints of usage, I received no high from the crack I purchased. It was as if the euphoric pleasure that I sought was now impossible to get. Though I received no euphoric lift, I remained tenacious in my pursuit. It seemed that my bondage to crack was so complete; that it was no longer required that Satan repay my efforts with euphoric pleasure. I felt as though he was saying, "You fool! I no longer need to draw you in by actual euphoric high— you only require the *idea* of high".

Some years earlier, at the home of my old friend Ben, I

found myself in the middle of someone's shoot out. As I was leaving his home after an unsuccessful day of cocaine pursuit, his friend Kirk, who happened to arrive hours earlier, expressed that he had a fall out with his surrogate son. I was about to start up my dad's 1980 red Ford Chevet when I observed a young man pull in front of the yard, Kirk simultaneously opening the front door, and each shooting at one another. I was in the midst of the fire. By the grace of God, I wasn't shot. The police were never notified, probably due to fear of reprisal. Both of those men are now dead. The older, Kirk, due to sickness— I suspect AIDS. And the younger was murdered—- gangland style. Notwithstanding these pivotal incidents, my pursuit of a daily high continued.

A short time later, I again entered into the Afton apartment complex. It was around midnight, and very few people were stirring. I felt more uncomfortable on this occasion than before. Earlier that week I prayed, with all earnestness, for strength to resist temptation, because I sensed a need for God's protection. Yet, I went out to get my high on. Upon parking, facing the exit of the darkened complex, I was approached by two young men. The first asked, "what ya need man?" I replied, "a $20 piece." He stated he could give me two "dime" pieces. As he ventured to put the pieces in my hand, one fell on the floor of my car. But he was very careful to give me only two rocks. I could see he had a gun on his side, but this, I thought, wasn't unusual for small time dealers at late night. Suddenly, the dealer accused me of not paying. At first, I couldn't understand why he said this thing, because we had exchanged the money and drugs simultaneously. He had the money clearly in his hand. I brought this fact to his immediate attention, but he refused to hear me. It was as if he couldn't focus on my voice, but only on his accusation of larceny. It seemed as though he had a prime directive, which was to kill me. Some youths seem to think that killing a person is a badge of honor. They feel compelled to commit the crime. The principality of the drug culture is truly controlled by Satan and his angels. And their human counterparts are moved to do that which their master, Satan, desires, which is to kill, steal, and destroy. His partner began whispering, "Shoot him, shoot!" He admonished him to shoot me at least three times. But something strange happened. I sensed an inner voice telling me "Do not look to your right." As I sensed a presence next to me, the voice spoke to my mind three times, and I obeyed. (Upon reflection, I wonder if it was the angels that visited Cathy and I during that high school class trip to Byrd Park, some twenty years earlier). So, the perpetrator, with the gun, began raising it to my car's window, on the driver's side, and peeked in as he prepared to shoot. But then, I saw his eyes widen as if they were going to pop out of their sockets. He had such a horrified look on his face as I've never seen in any horror movie. He ran from my car as if he was running to save his soul. His partner briefly peered through my window, and also took off running as if he was being chased by the death angel himself. I wasted no time in exiting that place. Making it home safely, and without injury, I waited until I was long out of Richmond before I looked squarely to my right. I did the drugs that I acquired on that night, but without any euphoric effects.

From that night, I sensed a continual fear in my spirit. For me, I sensed that death was imminent. For days I stayed home thinking about my mortality, but couldn't shake the feeling of death being near. I decided to pray with all my heart for answers to my plight of being unable to resist drugs, though I had a great desire to stop. I prayed, "Jesus, help me! Please give me an answer for this problem." I reminded God of the promises in His Word—to never leave me nor forsake me, and to deliver me from all unrighteousness.

Continuing to pray, I began sensing a gap in my spirit. It was as if there existed a place for the answer I needed, and

God was about to drop it into my spirit. Somehow, the bless-ing of God was upon me. I received unction to call Rev. Ray Smith, at the House of Life. I sensed that I must get a word from him before my answer could be completed. So, I dialed the phone, and Rev. Luster answered. He related that he would notify Rev. Smith to call me when he arrived. While waiting, I sensed that I should remain in prayer, praise, and worship until hearing from him. It is written in 1st **Thessalonians 5:16- 24** to *"Rejoice evermore. Pray with-out ceasing. In every thing give thanks: for this is the will of God in Christ Jesus concerning you. Quench not the Spirit. Despise not prophesying. Prove all things; hold fast that which is good. Abstain form all appearance of evil. And the God of peace sanctify you wholly; and I pray God your whole spirit and soul and body be preserved blame-less unto the coming of our Lord Jesus Christ. Faithful is he that calleth you, who also will do it"(KJV).* God's promises are secure in Christ Jesus, and His criteria for sanctification is plain and clear in those words.

Several hours later I received a call from Rev. Smith. I told him that I was holding on to God's promises, but my drug struggles remained very real. He spoke plain and brief. He said that I *must* be always mindful to do the right thing. I *must* put in action escape plans from the temptations that are to come, and decide once and for all whom I will serve! He expressed that Satan wanted to kill me, but my deliver-ance from the certain death of drug use was tied to an unyielding stance for Christ against the temptations of Satan, and that my commitment to Christ *must* be a life-long commitment. Rev. Smith admonished me to return to the after-care sessions at the House of Life.

After Rev. Smith hung up, I began receiving understand-ing from the Lord. The first thing He said to my spirit was, "David, I delivered you from drug addiction the very first time you asked." He said that the root of my problem was no longer drugging; for I wasn't experiencing a high anymore, which I had realized many months earlier. But, my root problem was that I had a false sense of commitment to Christ. The Lord related that I didn't understand my covenant with His Son. He reminded me of the situation he had with Peter denying Him three times. In the Gospel of St. John 13:37, Peter proclaims to Jesus that he will lay down his life for Christ. But Jesus recants Peter by prophesying that the cock shall not crow until he would deny Him three times (KJV). Jesus wanted Peter to know that he had a heart for Christ, but no commitment. However, Jesus was not finished with Peter. Although he was not yet ready to die for Christ, he would eventually settle it in his heart to be completely sold out for his Savior. The Bible says in St. John the 21st chapter that Jesus, after His resurrection, asked Peter three times to affirm his love for Him—the same number of times that Peter denied Him. Thus, Jesus, in return, affirmed Peter's commitment to die for Him. It is written in John 21:18-19 that Jesus prophesied of Peter that "....*when thou shalt be old, thou shalt stretch out thy hands, and another shall gird thee, and carry thee whither thou wouldest not. This spake he, signifying by what death he should glorify God. And when he had spoken this, he saith unto him, Follow me. (KJV)*

God did not speak to me on the same level as with Peter, but He made it clear that I must get to the point where I would rather die than sin against the Lord in such an abominable manner as drug sorcery. The Lord related that I had the capacity for deeper revelation of the true covenant between Christ, the bridegroom, and His Church, the bride. The kind of covenant that Christ has wrought in his body, as one bishop puts it, *is* a "DEATH COVENANT." A true marriage covenant is a holy and binding agreement between two heterosexual people or two entities, such as Christ and His Church, that professes love and trust for one another, to be honored even unto death. The Bible says in the epistle to the Ephesians 5th chapter that a husband ought to love his wife even as "Christ also loved the Church and gave himself for it." This death covenant relationship between Christ and the Church is a great mystery (Ephesians chapter 5), which the world cannot understand because it is spiritually discerned. Jesus Christ first set the standard, for He died for the sins of all that would receive His redemptive work on Calvary, and we must reciprocate. The Bible says that as disciples of Jesus Christ we are buried with Him, and are resurrected with Him. Christ is the first fruit of many Brethren. It was brought to my memory that which the Apostle Paul writes in his epistle to the Romans 12:1, ".... that ye present your bodies a living sacrifice, holy, acceptable unto God". I must be willing to die to the flesh, striving in obedience to Christ. As God stirred in my heart, He desired me to proclaim that I would rather die than sin against the Lord my God. And so I did. Does this mean that I would never again sin? No. But, it does mean that I would not again weaken to that previous strong hold of drug addiction.

I've been drug free for years, with many onslaught attacks, which the Lord allows for the edifying of my faith, and did allow in times past. I didn't know that in those temptations God was answering my prayer for greater faith. It is written in 1st Peter 1:6-7 that the temptations we endure are for our testing, so that we may be built up in the faith. So, I remember that which God has inspired me to never forget, that is, to confess the covenant I have with my Lord and Savior Jesus Christ, and to keep it! AMEN.

# The Present Day

The Lord has blessed me with the privilege of serving him in many capacities. He allows me to be the priest of God, in Christ, in my home. I am presently one of several associate ministers at my church— Little Elam Baptist Church. Also, the Lord has moved me to start and develop the "Eagles' Wings deliverance Ministry's Drug, alcohol, and Youth Mentorship Program". I am blessed, along with my wife Cathy, to home school our three young children, Jeremiah, Jacquelyn, and Jasmine. I follow, as often as possible, the "Promise Keepers" convention agenda. Their ministries are building a nation of Godly men to be used as vessels of the Lord in their homes, churches, and communities. Assuredly, It is well cemented in my spirit that I am no longer my own, but am brought with a price— the precious blood of the Lamb.

Of my many past friends and acquaintances, of only one do I have a testimony —my old friend Ben. Near the completion of this book, I saw him at a convenient store parking lot. He immediately began testifying of God's deliverance from cocaine. He shared with me how he was able to see the wasteland that drug abuse had made in the places that were under its principalities of darkness. Ben recognized that it only brought dysfunction and fruitless activity into his life. He confessed that the Lord had taken the taste of crack cocaine from his lips. Expressing that he struggles with other issues of life, he receives better understanding of God's will concerning those matters. Upon my last visit with Ben, prior to the completion of this book, we did something we never ventured to do over ten years of drugging together, we prayed. PRAISE GOD!

## "Psalm 2000"

As I stand in the midst of Your presence-
A whispering Spirit enters my mind;
Only to connect with my soul revealing infinite
Power only you can possess.
Yet gentle enough to subdue the most
turbulent of thoughts,
Which evolves through trials and tribulations
Molded by principalities of this world.
As the breath of Your wind touches my face, Love is
inhaled through my lungs-
Suddenly, my mind is transformed into a
state of peace and well-being,
As the Holy Spirit dwells within me-
Waiting to release the power of wisdom and truth
Used for the glory and honor of Your existence.
Still I am exposed to just a finite portion of
Your omnipotent presence.
How could I possibly contain all that you have to offer
In a single moment.

For Your power is so great
It could not possibly be measured by
human understanding.
A radiant beam descends from the sun;
An element so great, yet its warmth defines
Compassion upon my soul.
Your rain are tears of joy which helps us to grow.
How can we experience the colors of a rainbow
Without the shedding of a tear.
This could never compare to the blood that was shed
By our Lord and Savior.
Just one drop caused the earth to tremble;
Again revealing the almighty presence of Your power.
As another storm approaches,
May the roar of thunder remind the inhabitants
Of this land
That our King still sits on the throne.
May lightening extend power from heaven
And ignite the darkness of lifeless souls
That are so desperately in need of revival
and manna from heaven.
When this storm passes over
May the doors of heaven open up
And as your vision sets upon us,
May the glory of Your Spirit be able to say once again...
For I God created the heavens and the earth.
And it is ...very good.


Inspired by the Holy Spirit
Written by Blane Charity, Sr.

9 781591 606680